weeded 7/31/17

JAN 3 0 2015 DATE DUE

Handbook of Computer Troubleshooting

Michael Byrd
Jim Pearson
Robert A. Saigh

Glenlake Publishing Company, Ltd.
Chicago • London • New Delhi

Fitzroy Dearborn Publishers
Chicago and London

GPCo
1261 West Glenlake
Chicago, IL 60660
glenlake@ix.netcom.com

Table of Contents

About the Authors

Michael Byrd is an architect whose work includes residential, industrial, and commercial projects. He has integrated computers and computer networks into his design process to produce construction drawings, marketing presentations, graphic designs, three-dimensional models, and animations. He has worked as an educator at the Lubbock Science Spectrum and the Houston Museum of Natural Science. Mr. Byrd earned a Bachelor of Architecture degree from Texas Tech University.

Jim Pearson is a systems integrator and engineer who consults with companies who plan to implement e-business solutions. His expertise allows him to communicate effectively with a wide variety of personalities in the electronic world-from engineers and marketing experts to consumers and employees. He holds a B.A. in human and organizational development from Lindenwood University and an MS in education and instructional technology from Southern Illinois University at Edwardsville. Mr. Pearson currently teaches graduate courses in web development, media production management, management/administrative theory, organizational development, and personnel management and labor relations at Webster University and Lindenwood University.

Robert A. Saigh is a full-time writer with an extensive background in software training, technical writing, and editing and indexing. Mr. Saigh received his B.S. in communications and M.A.E. in English from Northwestern University in Evanston, Illinois. His previous book for Glenlake Publishing Company, Ltd., is *The International Dictionary of Data Communications*.

Preface

Creating a survival manual for computers is like trying to keep up with a rapidly accelerating train. The technology surges ahead; improvements are announced everyday.

Nonetheless, this *Handbook of Computer Troubleshooting* is as complete a guide as is feasible for the typical problems you'll run into most often. Both the neophyte and the experienced user will find plenty of useful tips to solve the more irksome yet common problems. We've included a list of company addresses and web sites to help you find hardware, software, peripherals, and more.

Now, and most important, here are our individual thanks:

Jim would like to thank everyone at KendallComm and at Acumen Consulting for continued help in researching and compiling this book.

Michael would like to thank everyone, but most especially his patient and inspiring wife, Tracey.

Rob would like to thank his always helpful guru extraordinaire, Grace McLoughlin, for information and minutiae that could not be found anywhere else and, of course, his wife, Jessica.

We all would like to thank everyone at Glenlake Publishing for their continued assistance and patience, especially Barbara Evans and Michael Jeffers. Thank you for waiting.

Disclaimer: The *Handbook of Computer Troubleshooting*, a general information book, has been compiled as painstakingly as possible. Still, new hardware, software, and technologies continue to be released steadily, making others obsolete.

With this in mind, we cannot insure that this information will apply to your particular situation and solve your particular conundrum. We have tried, to the best of our knowledge, to give you the best information available. Take the research in that context. Thank you.

Introduction

You may use this book, the *Handbook of Computer Troubleshooting*, in many ways. One approach is to read it straight through to get our information and advice. A second is to consider it a compendium, an adjunct to manuals and handbooks you may already have. The third, most efficacious, method is to go the chapter that will answer your question when you have the problem with your hardware, software, firmware, etc.

You can find the most common problems toward the front of the book. The idea is to help you discover some kind of answer within minutes since time has become so precious these days.

We have used the accepted conventions for this kind of work: for instance, if you see Alt+F, press the Alt and F buttons simultaneously. If you see, Alt, F, press the Alt button first and then the F button.

Contacting Us:
We have set up an e-mail address for you to send us your advice, discoveries, answers, and comments. We can then share this information with all our readers, so we will all benefit from your insight. If we use any of your contributions, we will credit you in the next edition of this book, though you will not receive any remuneration or rights.

If you have a tip, a comment, or a hint, please e-mail us at:

tihocs@yahoo.com

We will greatly appreciate your input and contributions.

The authors

Chapter 1
Hardware

INPUT DEVICES

Mice

So many types of mice and trackpads exist that we can cover only the most recurrent types and problems you may encounter. With most problems, first turn the monitor and computer off and back on. You can also solve many problems by calling the manufacturer or going to the manufacturer's web site; many sites offer troubleshooting information. Check all connections before assuming a worst-case scenario.

1. **My mouse has stopped responding, is sticky, or only likes moving in one direction (say, horizontally as opposed to vertically). What can I do about it?**

*   Check that all connections are still tight and the mouse cable is connected to the right port on the computer. If both mouse AND keyboard don't work, the computer has probably locked up, which means the mouse may be all right. Try the following:

    1. Turn off the computer and monitor completely.

2. Turn your mouse upside down, take out the trackball by twisting the door (usually counterclockwise), and remove the door to get to the ball.

3. Clean the trackball with soap and warm water. Avoid getting lint on the ball.

4. Inside the trackball holding area are two black rotating axles (perpendicular to one another) for horizontal and vertical screen movement and one white small axle (at a 45 degree angle to the other axles for diagonal movement). Remove dirt from the center of the white axle and the sides of the black ones by gently scraping it off with a fingernail or use a cotton swab with cleaning liquid.

5. You can also clean the area with compressed air but do this gently.

6. Replace the trackball.

7. Close the trackball door.

8. Turn the monitor and computer back on.

9. Test the mouse on a smooth surface, preferably a mouse pad.

HINT 1: Think of any mouse whether with a top trackball (like Microsoft's EasyBall) or a bottom trackball (like the standard PS/2 mouse) as a manual floor sweeper. Whatever the ball of the mouse comes in contact with may be swept into the innards of the device. If you eat while working at any computer, grease from your fingers or small particles of food may begin to interfere with mouse operation. Therefore:

- Keep the mousepad clean and dustless.

- Don't eat anything while working at the computer.

- Don't drink anything unless the liquid is in a sealed container. I like to keep what I'm drinking in a travel mug or the kind of bottle bicyclists use (and I keep the container on the floor).

- Buy a can of compressed air and clean the keyboard and mouse periodically—but only when the computer is turned off.

HINT 2: Learn to use more keyboard commands; these are faster than a mouse and useful in case of mouse emergencies. Experiment with the command keys (F1 through F12) and combinations of the command keys with Alt, Shift, and Ctrl keys, etc. Create a list of these commands to keep handy. I can get all of my e-mail without ever using the mouse. Think of that as a useful possibility—or a challenge.

Definitions:

A Trackball: Looks like an upside-down mouse with a large ball facing up. EasyBall is one example. Some people prefer the trackball because it reduces arm and wrist motion.

2. My mouse in Windows 3.x will not respond at all. What can I do about it?

- If the mouse is moving but the buttons are not responding, perhaps someone has switched your left and right buttons. To fix this:

    1. Double-click on the Main icon, the Control Group icon, and then the Mouse icon.

    2. Make sure the Swap Left/Right Buttons checkbox has not been checked (Alt+S).

    3. If the Swap Left/Right Buttons checkbox has been set for a left-handed person, switch back to right-handed use, or vice versa (Alt+R or Alt+L).

3. My mouse in Windows 95 will not respond at all. What can I do about it?

- If the mouse is moving but the buttons are not responding, perhaps someone has switched your left and right buttons. To fix this:

    1. Click on the Start button, Settings, and then Control Panel.

    2. Click on the Mouse icon.

3. Click on the Buttons tab.

4. If Button configuration has been set for a left-handed person and you're right-handed, switch it by pressing Alt+R; if you want to set it for left-handed use, press Alt+L.

• If the mouse buttons have not been switched but are still not responding, the buttons themselves may be dead. Borrow a friend's mouse and see if it works. If it does, your own mouse is dead and must be replaced. (Since standard mice are cheap, it's a good idea to have a spare around at all times.)

• If you have just bought the mouse, make sure the connection to the port does not need an additional piece. For instance, Synaptics had an ergonomic keyboard that required an interconnection piece (serial to PS/2 connector) for some mice but not others. To see if you have the correct mouse device selected:

1. Press the Start button.

2. Type the letter s (for Settings), or use the up arrow key to maneuver to Settings.

3. Type the letter c (for Control Panel), or use the right arrow key (and press the Enter button).

4. Use the down and right/left arrow keys to maneuver to the System icon(or, quickly type the letters s and then y to get to the System icon).

5. Press the Enter button once the icon has been highlighted (dark blue).

6. Use the Ctrl+Tab buttons to go to the Device Manager tab (second tab).

7. Press the Tab button.

8. Use the down arrow key to go to Mouse (or, quickly type the three letters m, o, and then u,).

9. Press the right arrow key.

10. Press the down arrow key to highlight your mouse device.

11. Press the Tab button (to highlight the Properties button below).

12. Press Enter.

13. Press the Ctrl+Tab buttons to go to the Driver tab (second tab).

14. If the listed mouse device does not match what you have, call your place of purchase and ask which mouse device should be listed and how to get it. Or, call the mouse manufacturer direct-ly and ask the same questions.

4.   My mouse will still not respond. What can I do?

- If the mouse is neither moving nor clicking, perhaps the computer has lost the drivers for the mouse. To check this, do the following:

  1. Save whatever document you were working on before shutting the system down. If you cannot save with the mouse, use key-board functions such as Alt+F followed by clicking on the S key (S=Save for most Windows programs).

  2. Turn off the computer completely, wait about fifteen seconds, and turn it back on to see if the problem goes away.

- If the first step proves unsuccessful, see if you have the correct vir-tual mouse driver, usually named vmouse.vxd, lmouse.vxd, msmouse.vxd, or a special company abbreviation with the .vxd extension. These files can usually be found in the Windows (or Windows.000) folder using Windows Explorer or My Computer. In Windows 3.1, the file is usually mouse.drv, found by using File Manager. To check the mouse driver in Windows 95:

  1. Press the Start button

  2. Type the letter s (for Settings), or use the up arrow key to maneu-ver to Settings.

3. Type the letter c (for Control Panel), or use the right arrow key (and press the Enter button).

4. Use the down and right/left arrow keys to maneuver to the System icon (or, quickly type the letters s and then y to get to the System icon.

5. Press the Enter button once the icon has been highlighted (dark blue).

6. Use the Ctrl+Tab buttons to go to the Device Manager tab (second tab).

7. Click on the Driver tab at the top of the dialog box. This driver dialog box will show what kind of driver you have; you will probably be able either to see Driver file details or Update driver.

8. Use the down arrow key to go to Mouse (or, quickly type the three letters m, o, and then u,).

9. Press the right arrow key.

10. Press the down arrow key to highlight your mouse device.

11. Press the Tab button (to highlight the Properties button below).

12. Press Enter.

13. Press the Ctrl+Tab buttons to go to the Driver tab (second tab). This driver dialog box will show what kind of driver you have.

14. To see what kind of driver you have, press the Tab button to activate the Driver File Details...button and press the Enter button.

15. Or, if you wish to update the driver, press the Tab button to go to the Update Driver...button and press the Enter button. You must have a CD-ROM or floppy disk that contains the new driver. If not, download the updated driver from the manufacturer's web site via the Internet. Once you have the correct file, press the Tab button to get to the Update Driver button and follow instructions.

Definitions:

Driver (also called Device Driver): A software program that allows the hardware peripherals to talk to the computer. This program tells the peripheral (mouse, keyboard, etc.) what your instructions mean (for instance, when typing the letter A or moving the mouse and clicking).

Virtual Device Driver (VxD or vxd): These virtual drivers mimic buffers between your hardware and software. With so much information flying around in the computer at lightning speed, the VxD ensures that the right data reach the correct software. (Ever thought about how an Excel file knows to go to the Excel program?) Occasionally, you will see other designations, such as VmD. The middle letter can indicate the type of hardware, e.g., "m" for mouse, and so on.

5. My mouse pointer does not appear when I turn on the computer. What can I do about it?

- Turn off the computer and monitor completely, wait at least twenty seconds, and turn both back on.

- If the mouse pointer does not appear, use your keyboard commands (learn them before this happens) and go to the Device Manager to see if your mouse is still alive and well. Use the Alt+(letter) buttons in conjunction with the arrow buttons to move to the System icon. Use Ctrl+Tab buttons to switch between tab folders. To get to the Device Manager:

  1. Press the Start button

  2. Type the letter s (for Settings), or use the up arrow key to maneuver to Settings.

  3. Type the letter c (for Control Panel), or use the right arrow key (and press the Enter button).

  4. Use the down and right/left arrow keys to maneuver to the System icon (or, quickly type the letters s and then y to get to the System icon.

  5. Press the Enter button once the icon has been highlighted (dark blue).

6. Use the Ctrl+Tab buttons to go to the Device Manager tab (second tab).

7. Click on the Driver tab at the top of the dialog box. This driver dialog box will show what kind of driver you have; you will probably be able either to see Driver file details or Update driver.

8. Use the down arrow key to go to Mouse (or, quickly type the three letters m, o, and then u,).

9. Press the right arrow key.

10. Press the down arrow key to highlight your mouse device.

11. Press the Tab button (to highlight the Properties button below).

12. Press Enter.

13. Press the Ctrl+Tab buttons to go to the Driver tab (second tab). This driver dialog box will show what kind of driver you have.

14. To see what kind of driver you have, press the Tab button to activate the Driver File Details...button and press the Enter button.

15. Or, if you wish to update the driver, press the Tab button to go to the Update Driver...button and press the Enter button. You must have a CD-ROM or floppy disk that contains the new driver. If not, download the updated driver from the manufacturer's web site via the Internet. Once you have the correct file, press the Tab button to get to the Update Driver button and follow instructions.

• Have you installed any other peripherals? Sometimes, when you install a new device (tape drive, etc.), the computer experiences an Interrupt ReQuest (IRQ) conflict as two devices try to share the same port. You will probably have to re-install the new peripheral. The most common effect of this conflict is Windows freezing when you try to use the mouse. If you're still a DOS user, type in MSD (for Microsoft Diagnostics) at the C:/prompt to determine what devices you have and whether there is a conflict.

- Your cables may be bad. If the cable is bad, you'll need to buy a new one. Switch yours with a friend's, turn the computer completely off and then on, and see if the problem disappears.

- The port connection could be old and not making contact, so the mouse signal is not reaching the computer. As your computer is booting, watch for a list of installed hardware (also found in Device Manager).

- Your mouse could have died a quiet death. Since mice are usually inexpensive, replace the mouse (use that spare one).

- Maybe a fuse has burned out on the motherboard, the jumper settings have been changed, or a virus has gotten into the system. A host of problems (too numerous to mention) could be working here. Consult with your favorite guru, technicians at the store from which you bought the computer or device, or the manufacturer.

Definitions:

Interrupt ReQuest (IRQ): A communication route designed to carry signals to tell the computer to stop its current activity and wait for further instructions. Each device has its own IRQ; the higher numbers get priority first. If a hard drive has IRQ14 and the mouse IRQ12, the hard drive is taken care of first.

6. Why do I want a trackpad also called a touchpad?

If you have any kind of repetitive motion disorder, such as carpal tunnel syndrome, touchpads are better for your fingers and hands because no clicking is required (see chapter 5 on ergonomics for more detail). Many allow vertical zooming movements if you simply keep your finger on the pad. Others allow you to switch between the touchpad and a mouse (if you wish to have one). Most touchpads are part of the keyboard (the best are in the middle toward the front) but they can be separate (external). External ones are good for moving around your desk but the internal ones take up less space.

Definitions:

Trackpad: A trackpad is the square you see as part of a keyboard on which you glide your finger. As you move your finger, the screen pointer will also move. Single or double-tapping the pad is equivalent to clicking or double-clicking a mouse.

7. I have a trackpad and am having some of the same problems as were mentioned with the mouse. What can I do?

- As always, check all connections to ensure they're tight and making contact.

- Since a trackpad has no moving parts, cleaning is greatly reduced.

- Still, keep the pad clean and clean it with a damp cloth when the computer is turned off.

- Keep food and drink away from the pad and the keyboard at all times.

- If the mouse symbol is moving but the buttons are not responding, they may be either switched or the buttons themselves may be dead. To check if the buttons have been switched:

  1. Press the Start button

  2. Type the letter s (for Settings), or use the up arrow key to maneuver to Settings.

  3. Type the letter c (for Control Panel), or use the right arrow key (and press the Enter button).

  4. Use the down and right/left arrow keys to maneuver to the Mouse icon (or, quickly type the letters m, o, and then u to get to the Mouse icon).

  5. Press the Enter button once the icon has been highlighted (dark blue).

6. You will automatically be in the Buttons tab.

7. Check to determine whether the right mouse button (Alt+R) or the left mouse button (Alt+L) has been selected. Sometimes, in work situations, a left-handed person has borrowed a right-handed person's computer (or, vice versa) and forgot to switch the buttons back to their original function.

• Make sure you have the correct driver for the trackpad. To determine what mouse and driver you have:

1. Press the Start button

2. Type the letter s (for Settings), or use the up arrow key to maneuver to Settings.

3. Type the letter c (for Control Panel), or use the right arrow key (and press the Enter button).

4. Use the down and right/left arrow keys to maneuver to the System icon (or, quickly type the letters s and then y to get to the System icon.

5. Press the Enter button once the icon has been highlighted (dark blue).

6. Use the Ctrl+Tab buttons to go to the Device Manager tab (second tab).

7. Click on the Driver tab at the top of the dialog box. This driver dialog box will show what kind of driver you have; you will probably be able either to see Driver file details or Update driver.

8. Use the down arrow key to go to Mouse (or, quickly type the three letters m, o, and then u,).

9. Press the right arrow key.

10. Press the down arrow key to highlight your mouse device.

11. Press the Tab button (to highlight the Properties button below).

12. Press Enter.

13. Press the Ctrl+Tab buttons to go to the Driver tab (second tab). This driver dialog box will show what kind of driver you have.

14. To see what kind of driver you have, press the Tab button to activate the Driver File Details...button and press the Enter button.

15. Or, if you wish to update the driver, press the Tab button to go to the Update Driver...button and press the Enter button. You must have a CD-ROM or floppy disk that contains the new driver. If not, download the updated driver from the manufacturer's web site via the Internet. Once you have the correct file, press the Tab button to get to the Update Driver button and follow instructions.

8. I hate my mouse (or trackpad) and/or pointer. How do I make it easier to use?

• To alter appearances or usage characteristics:

1. Click on Start button, Settings, and then Control Panel.

2. Double-click on the Mouse icon.

3. Click on the various tabs to alter options such as for swapping left and right buttons, double-clicking speed, type of pointers, tracking speed, mouse trails, and more.

See the following questions for detailed instructions on changing characteristics.

9. How do I swap the left and right mouse buttons in Windows 3.x?

• To swap the buttons:

1. Double-click on the Main group icon, Control Panel icon, and then Mouse icon.

2. Click on the Swap Left/Right Buttons checkbox (or use your Alt commands).

10. How do I swap the left and right mouse buttons in Windows 95?

* To swap the buttons:

   1. Click on the Start button, Settings, and then Control Panel.

   2. Double-click on the Mouse icon.

   3. Click on the Buttons tab.

   4. Click on the Left-handed or Right-handed radio buttons.

11. How do I alter the mouse's double-clicking speed in Windows 3.x?

* To change your mouse's double-clicking speed in Windows 3.x:

   1. Double-click on the Main group icon, the Control Panel icon, and then the Mouse icon.

   2. Drag the checkbox under Double Click Speed.

   3. Click on the Test button to ensure you are comfortable with the new speed.

12. How do I alter the mouse's double-clicking speed in Windows 95?

* To change your mouse's double-clicking speed in Windows 95:

   1. Click on the Start button, Settings, and then Control Panel.

   2. Double-click on the Mouse icon.

   3. Click on the Buttons tab.

4. Alter the speed by adjusting the horizontal marker in the Buttons tab.

5. Test your new setting by double-clicking on the Jack-in-the-Box symbol (for Windows) before approving the new setting. If you can get Jack to pop out of his box, you have a good speed.

6. Click on the Apply button to make the new setting permanent.

NOTE: Clicking on the Apply button approves the new setting without kicking you out of the dialog box. If you click on OK, you will be unceremoniously booted out of this dialog box and will have to click on its icon if you want to return.

13. I want a different pointer. How do I change pointers?

Many people prefer a larger pointer because they can see it more easily. Some like to discard the hourglass symbol with piano keys moving or the horse galloping. Whatever symbol you desire, make sure it's useful to your daily tasks.

You can change the types of pointers by using the Pointers tab of the Mouse dialog box. If you double-click on the busy hourglass symbol in the lower part of the Pointers tab window, other choices will pop up, on which you may double-click. Remember: If you don't click on OK or Apply (or you do click on Cancel), none of your new settings will be memorized.

You cannot easily change the look of the pointer in Windows 3.x. To change your pointer in Windows 95:

1. Click on the Start button, Settings, and then Control Panel.

2. Double-click on the Mouse icon.

3. Click on the Pointers tab.

4. Double-click on the pointer you wish to change.

5. Double-click on the pointer you wish to use.

6. Click on Save.

14. How do I change the mouse's tracking speed in Windows 3.x?

You've got all the settings right where you want them, but the darned pointer just will not move across the screen quickly. Or, maybe it's moving too quickly. To change the speed:

1. Double-click on the Main group icon, the Control Panel icon, and then the Mouse icon.

2. Drag the checkbox horizontally under the heading of Mouse Tracking Speed.

15. How do I change the mouse's tracking speed in Windows 95?

You've got all the settings right where you want them, but the darned pointer just will not move across the screen quickly. Or, maybe it's moving too quickly. Generally, people who play computer games want the fastest speed. To change the speed:

1. Click on the Start button, Settings, and then Control Panel.

2. Double-click on the Mouse button.

3. Click on the Motion tab.

4. Under the Pointer heading, drag the dial horizontally in the direction you want to go.

5. Click on the Apply button to keep the new setting if you want to stay in the dialog box.

6. Click on the OK button to keep the new setting if you're ready to leave the dialog box.

16. I want to change the pointer trails. How do I do this in Windows 3.x?

You either hate or love these. To heighten mouse visibility, you can add trails (looking like ghost images) that appear when you move the mouse. You cannot adjust the amount of mouse trails in Windows 3.x, but you can in Windows 95. To add or delete mouse trails:

1. Click on the Main group icon, Control Panel icon.

2. Double-click on the Mouse icon.

3. Click on the Mouse Trails checkbox.

17. I want to change the pointer trails. How do I do this in Windows 95?

You either hate or you love these. To further heighten mouse visibility, you can add trails (looking like ghost images) that appear when you move the mouse. You can also adjust the amount of trails. To do either:

1. Click on the Start button, Settings, and then Control Panel.

2. Double-click on the Mouse icon.

3. Click on the Show pointer trails checkbox.

4. Drag the pointer horizontally between Short and Long.

5. Click on the Apply button to keep the new setting and stay in the dialog box.

6. Click on the OK button to keep the new setting and leave the dialog box.

18. I hate mice and pads. Can't I use something else?

Yes. You can dictate to the computer and let it do all the typing for you. Many voice-recognition software packages exist (such as Naturally Speaking from Dragon Software. You need to train them to recognize your voice, so allow plenty of time to get the system usable, and make sure you have enough hard drive space, a fast enough computer, and enough Random Access Memory (RAM) to make them work efficiently, or your computer will not be able to keep up with you as you speak.

When you were using the keyboard and mouse, you could talk on the phone or listen to music at the same time. You cannot do that with voice-recognition software. If your microphone hears this background noise, it will type it in. The last thing you need in your thermodynamics thesis is the baseball announcement: "And it's outta here!"

These software packages keep improving and coming out constantly. Check out company web sites, see if you can see them demonstrated somewhere (at a store or a computer convention), and decide whether voice-recognition software is worth your investment of time and money.

19. I'm physically challenged and can't use a mouse. What do you recommend?

You can use voice-recognition software or, in Windows, you can use the Accessibility Options, which allow you to use the keyboard to control the mouse functions. To get to the Accessibility Options, do the following:

1. Click on the Start button, Settings, and then Control Panel.

2. Double-click on the Accessibility Options icon.

3. Once in this dialog box, use the various selections to customize your mouse accessibility. Experimentation is the key here.

Keyboards

Keyboards have come a long way from the stodgy take-it-or-leave-it models to the ergonomic ones with adjustable split keyboards, contoured keyboards, floating arm keyboards, touchpads, and more.

As to the kind of keyboard to buy, consult chapter 5 on ergonomics. Still, follow some general basics of operation. The keyboard should be at elbow height. In other words, you should not have to raise or lower your arms to work; the keyboard should act as a natural extension of your body. If not, lower the keyboard table, raise your chair, or both. To check the alignment, make sure your forearms are parallel to the ground. Take frequent breaks, stretch your fingers, and shake out your fingers to avoid problems.

Keyboards don't require much care. Our advice is simple:

- No food and no drink near the keyboard, mouse, or any other hardware, for that matter.

- Buy covers for the keyboard, monitor, and other external hardware like printers.

- Read the instructions.

- Keep all 800 manufacturer numbers handy in a file (not on a disk). Know what brand and model you have in case you have to call the manufacturer, the store, or the guru.

- Keep a couple of cans of compressed air around to clean the keyboard, mouse, and tops of components. Make sure you get the cans with the long, thin, red tubes to direct the air precisely, so you can clean between the keys.

20. I'm typing but nothing is happening on the screen. What should I do?

- Does the mouse work? If the mouse works, then the computer may not have locked up.

- If the computer has locked up, turn the computer and monitor off completely. Don't select Restart but choose Shut down. Keep the computer off for at least 20 seconds. Turn the computer back on and see if the problem is gone.

- Check all cable connections to ensure they're snug and tight. Check the pins to make sure they're not bent or broken.

- If the problem persists, test the keyboard on another computer. Also, test another cable connector. This can isolate what could be wrong.

- Ensure that the correct drivers are loaded. To check your drivers in Windows 95, do the following:

  1. Click on the Start button, Settings, Control Panel, and then the System icon.

  2. Click on the + sign next to Keyboard.

  3. Click on the keyboard model.

  4. Click on the Properties button.

  5. Click on the Drivers tab to see if you have a driver and/or need one.

- If the keyboard doesn't respond to your attempts to revive it, it's possible its encoder circuitry was blown by a static charge. Get in the habit of touching something else metallic before touching the computer and its peripherals.

21. I have spilled some liquid on the keyboard. What should I do now?

- If you spill liquid on the keyboard:

  1. Immediately save any files you're working on.

  2. Turn the computer and monitor off (and keep them off).

  3. Gently pull off one key at a time. The space bar has two connections, so pull this off carefully. Remember where each key goes.

  4. Clean underneath and around each key with cotton swabs and an alcohol-based product like isopropyl.

  5. Let the keyboard completely dry before reassembling and using.

22. The keys keep getting sticky. How can I stop this?

- Turn the computer off, hold the keyboard vertically and tilted forward so that particles will fall out, and clean it with compressed air.

Blow the air (with a long red nozzle extension) carefully. Turn the computer back on to see if this has solved the problem.

- Check the sensitivity of the keyboard setting. To check sensitivity in Windows 3.X:

  1. Click on the Main group icon, and then the Control Panel icon.

  2. Double-click the Keyboard icon.

  3. Click and drag the square cursor under Delay Before First Repeat or under Repeat Rate.
  4. Type in the test area to see if you like your new setting.

  5. Click on OK.

- To check sensitivity in Windows 95:

  1. Click on the Start button, Settings, and then the Control Panel.

  2. Double-click on the Keyboard icon.

  3. Click on the Speed tab.

  4. Drag the square underneath Repeat delay or Repeat rate.

  5. Click in the Click here and hold down a key to test repeat rate; try typing letters with your new setting.

  6. Click on Apply if you want to save the new settings and stay in the dialog box.

  7. Click on OK if you're finished with the dialog box.

23. My keyboard is duplicating letters as I type. What do I do?

The speed of your keyboard needs to be adjusted.

- To adjust the keyboard speed in Windows 3.x:

  1. Double-click on the Main group icon, the Control Panel icon, and then the Keyboard icon.

  2. Drag the square cursor under Delay Before First Repeat or under Repeat Rate.

  3. Type in the test area to see if you like your new setting.

  4. Click on OK.

- To adjust the keyboard speed in Windows 95:

  1. Click on the Start button, Settings, and then the Control Panel.

  2. Double-click on the Keyboard icon.

  3. Click on the Speed tab.

  4. Drag the square underneath Repeat delay or Repeat rate.

  5. Click on Click here and hold down a key to test the repeat rate; try typing letters with your new setting.

  6. Click on Apply if you want to save the new settings and stay in the dialog box.

  7. Click on OK if you're finished with the dialog box.

24. I hate using my mouse all the time. Can I do something else?

Yes. You can use your keyboard to navigate. Some ways to do it are:

- To manipulate an active window in Windows 3.x or Windows 95:

  1. Press the Alt button and, while holding it down, press the Spacebar (Alt+Spacebar).

2. Type n (no capitalization needed) to minimize the window (Alt+Space, n), or type x (no capitalization needed) to maximize the window (Alt+Space, x).

• To close an active window in Windows 3.x or Windows 95:'

  1. Press Alt and, while holding it down, press the Spacebar (Alt+Spacebar).

  2. Type c (no capitalization needed) to close the window (Alt+Spacebar, c), or press the Alt button and while holding it down press F4 (Alt+F4).

• To open Windows Explorer in Windows 95:

  1. Right-click on the Start button and select Explorer, or

  2. Simultaneously press the Explorer button and the letter e.

• To go through all the active applications in Windows 3.x:

  1. Hold down the Alt button.

  2. Keep clicking the Tab button until you reach the application you're looking for.

  3. Release the Tab button.

• To go through all the active applications in Windows 95:

  1. Hold down the Alt button.

  2. Keep clicking the Tab button until you reach the application you're looking for.

  3. Release the Tab button.

• To cycle through all the group icons in Windows 3.x:

  1. Hold down the Ctrl button.

2. Keep clicking on the Tab button (Ctrl+Tab) until you reach the group you're looking for.

3. Press the Enter button.

- To close group icons that are open in Windows 3.x:

  1. Click and hold the Ctrl button.

  2. Then click the F4 button (Ctrl+F4).

- To shut down Windows 3.x:

  1. Click and hold the Alt button.

  2. Click on the F4 button (Alt+F4).

25. I keep hearing about the Ctrl+Alt+Del sequence. What is it?

- In Windows 3.x, if you press and hold the Ctrl, Alt, and Del buttons (so all three are now pressed), you restart the computer. You will not get a warning.

- In Windows 95, if you press and hold the Ctrl, Alt, and Del buttons (so all three are now pressed), you activate the Close Program dialog box. This allows you to close an individual program (pressing the End Task button), especially if it has locked up. If you execute the Ctrl+Alt+Del sequence a second time, you will restart the computer; you will not get a warning.

CAUTION: You could possibly lose all information doing this sequence.

26. I hate keyboards. Can I do something else?

You don't have to use either the mouse or the keyboard. You can dictate to the computer and let it do all the typing for you. Voice recognition software packages like Naturally Speaking from Dragon Software do need to be "trained" to your voice. Make sure you have enough space on the hard drive, a fast enough computer, and enough RAM to make them work efficiently; if not, your computer will not be able to keep up with you as you speak.

When you were using the keyboard and mouse, you could talk on the phone or listen to music while you worked. You cannot do that with voice recognition software. If your microphone hears background noise, it will try to type it. The last thing you need in your thermodynamics article is a baseball announcement: "And it's outta here."

These software packages keep improving constantly. Check out company web sites, see if you can see them demonstrated at a store or a computer convention, and decide for yourself.

27. I don't want voice recognition software. What other kinds of keyboards exist?

Yes, you can get adjustable split keyboards for $100 to $500. Some of these attach to your chair arms so your hands and arms rest on the armrest. Others split the keyboard in half and allow you to adjust the angle of the split, which is great for people who are taller, have large fingers, etc. Still others don't split the keyboard but contour the keys to match the curve your fingers create because the thumb and the pinkie are shorter than the three middle fingers.

Consult our ergonomics and address chapter for more information.

28. I'm physically challenged and can't use a keyboard. What do you suggest?

You have the option of voice-recognition software, and in Windows, you can use the Accessibility Options, which allow you to use the keyboard to control the mouse functions. To access these options:

1. Click on Start, Settings, Control Panel, and the Accessibility Options icon.

2. Once in the dialog box, use the various selections to customize your mouse accessibility.

Experimentation is the key here.

Windows 3.x (standard installation) does not have accessibility options.

Monitors

Monitors have advanced rapidly from monochrome displays (MDA: monochrome display adapter) to flat screens with speakers, auxiliary ports, and more.

You can solve many monitor problems by calling the manufacturer or going to the manufacturer's web site, which often has information on error codes and other troubleshooting.

To clear offending data, begin by turning the monitor on and off. Then turn the computer on and off. Check all connections before assuming a worst-case scenario.

For each of the problems below, start by making sure you have the correct monitor selected for your computer. Before you begin the process, have the CD-ROM or floppy disk with the appropriate files ready:

1. Click on the Start button, Settings, and then Control Panel.

2. Double-click on the Display icon.

3. Click on Settings.

4. Click on Advanced Properties.

5. Click on the Monitor tab

6. Click on the Change button. If the wrong monitor is selected, change the brand and model.

29. Can you give me some general advice about monitor maintenance?

If you've read the preceding sections, these recommendations will sound familiar:

- No food or drink near the monitor. In fact, no food or drink near the keyboard, mouse, or any other hardware or software.

- Buy covers for the monitor, keyboard, and other external hardware devices like printers.

- Read all instructions carefully.

- Have all manufacturer phone numbers handy and in a file—not on a disk.

- Keep the brand, model, and serial number handy in case you have to call the manufacturer or store.

- Have cans of compressed air around to clean the top of the monitor. Make sure you get the cans with the long, thin, red tubes to direct the air precisely into any tight places.

- Only clean components when the entire system is turned off.

- Never use unshielded cable for connections.

30. Can you give me some general advice on how to set up the monitor?

Consult chapter 5 on ergonomics first and then make sure:

- The middle of the monitor is at the same height as your eyes. If not, raise the monitor with risers, lower the desk, adjust your chair, or do whatever combination of these gets the monitor to the right place.

- The monitor is at arm's length or at least three feet away. The monitor is like a TV, so don't sit too close.

- Have adequate lighting with no glare on the screen.

31. My monitor is blank (or black). What can I do?

- Check that the monitor is on, and the power is reaching the monitor. If the fuse in the power strip is dead (e.g., from a power surge), replace the fuse and try the monitor and computer again.

- Plug the monitor into a different outlet to isolate as many variables as possible.

- Check whether a screen saver or power saver is on (most monitors with power saver options have an Energy Star icon on the front). The power saver will seem to shut the monitor down if the computer is on and the system has not been used for a specified time. Also, some people select a "Blank Screen" screen saver that has the same effect as a power saver.

Definitions:

Energy Star: A program created by the Environmental Protection Agency (EPA) to encourage hardware that is more efficient and appliances. To display the star, the product must meet minimum EPA requirements. The device must know to power down when not in use after a certain period without losing any current information. The device must also power down to 30 or fewer watts of power.

32. How do I adjust the screen saver in Windows?

To adjust the screen saver in Windows 3.1:

1. Double-click on the Main group icon, Control Panel, and then the Desktop icon.

2. Adjust the screen saver (by type, time limit, and individual characteristics.

To adjust the screen saver in Windows 95:

1. Click on Start, Settings, and then Control Panel.

2. Double-click on the Display icon.

3. Click on the Screen Saver tab.

4. Change the screen saver and its characteristics. In the Wait checkbox or spinner, select how many minutes must elapse before it starts—a reasonable amount of time is ten to 15 minutes.

5. If necessary, adjust the energy saving feature of the monitor here. If you choose "Low-power standby," the monitor will make the screen go blank. If you choose "Shut off monitor," the computer will do that instead.

CAUTION: You can add a password here but don't do it. Why? What if you go to lunch, and when you get back you've forgotten the screensaver password? If so, you will have to turn the computer off, lose whatever you were working on, and start again. And how many passwords do you want to have to remember?

33. My screen is still blank (or black). What can I do?

• Check all cable connections to see they're snug and fitting tightly into the sockets. (If you want to pull the cable out, turn off the monitor and computer first.)

• Look to see if the cable pins are not aligned.

• Check the pins in the connection in the computer.

• Switch cables.

34. The display colors aren't balanced. What can I do?

Did you just buy the monitor? Were the colors askew when you plugged it in? If so, take it back and ask the store to adjust the monitor settings before you change something to a more degraded state. Otherwise:

• Turn the monitor and computer off. Restart them to see if the problem goes away.

• If the color looks bad but no single complete color is missing, try the Red-Green-Blue (RGB) adjustments. Write down or remember the settings before you begin to change them in case you need to return them to their original settings. With older monitors, you may have to take the cover off to get to the RGB dials.

CAUTION: Don't take the cover off the monitor. Even unplugged the monitor has hazardous voltages inside. And opening the monitor cover may void the warranty.

35. My monitor appears to be missing one primary (Red-Green-Blue: RGB) color. What can I do?

* Check the cables.

* Look to see if the pins are bent or missing. I had one monitor with a 15-pin connection. Pins 1, 2, and 3 were Red, Green, and Blue. Pins 6, 7, and 8 were for RGB return signals (this is where the manufacturer's manual comes in handy). One of the pins was missing and that was color. If you work at a company where the help desk holds all the manuals, ask for a photocopy of the key pages for your components in case problems like this occur and you have no one to ask.

* Turn off the computer and monitor and switch the cables.

* If that doesn't help, connect the monitor to another computer or connect someone else's monitor to your computer. If the other monitor has the same color distortion, the problem is in the computer.

* The color input may not be terminated. Don't worry about what this means, but if you have a manual, make sure you see "75 ohm positive" listed for analog signals. If this signal is terminated, you'll have color problems. Check with the manufacturer or the store where you bought it.

CAUTION: Don't take the cover off the monitor. Even unplugged the monitor has hazardous voltages inside. And opening the monitor cover may void the warranty.

36. The display is distorted. What can I do?

* Check cables, monitor power plug, etc.

* Turn off any room or desk lights to see if the problem disappears. Fluorescent lights are notorious for causing distortions.

* Turn off any radios or televisions. They can cause electrical interference.

* Turn off any fans.

- Try your surge protector in a different wall outlet.

- Use your degaussing or pincushioning correction capabilities by pressing those buttons or switches to see if they reduce the distortion. (Consult your manual for the location of these buttons.)

- Try turning the monitor in a different direction. A different orientation may be enough to reduce the distortion.

- Press the refresh button or switch (if the monitor has one).

- You may have an incorrectly configured onboard video card. If you aren't sure, check with the manufacturer or the store where you bought it. Or, call your computer guru or the help desk.

Definitions:

Barrel distortion: A visual warping in which the left and right sides of the screen seem to bend outward from the center.

Pincushioning: A visual warping in which the left and right sides of the screen seem to bend inward to the center.

37. The display looks like a broadcast scrambled by a local cable company. What can I do?

- Turn the monitor and computer completely off and then back on.

- Press the Refresh button, if there is one.

- Check the cable, pins, and connections.

- If you have a technician on hand, ask him to check the sync polarity, signal rates, and signal lengths.

- Do the steps listed in answer to question 36.

- Check the Refresh setting. To do this:

  1. Click on Start, Programs, and then Windows Explorer.

2. Click on the Windows or Windows.000 folder of your hard drive.

3. Scroll down on the right until you reach the Regedit (Registry Editor) file.

4. Double-click on the Regedit icon.

5. Click on the + sign next to the HKEY_LOCAL_MACHINE folder.

6. Click on the + sign next to the System folder.

7. Click on the + sign next to the CurrentControlSet folder.

8. Click on the + sign next to the Control folder.

9. Click on the Update folder.

10. Change the value of UpdateMode to 00, which forces Refresh to its fastest rate.

CAUTION: Remember the original rate in case you need to reuse it.

38. The display is rolling or scrolling up or down verti- cally. What can I do?

• Check the vertical button or switch at the front of the monitor and adjust the speed of the vertical image movement.

• Check the wiring, cable connections, pins, etc.

39. The image has a ghost. What can I do?

• Replace your cable with another cable.

• If the new cable doesn't help, consider a more expensive super-shielded VGA cable. These cables have shielded coax conductors that almost always reduces or stops ghosting.

Definition:

Video Graphics Array (VGA): A monitor developed by IBM that can display up to 640 pixels by 480 pixels. If you reduce the resolution, you can increase the number of colors—an unacceptable tradeoff, however, because SVGA monitors exist. Older VGA versions are Color Graphics Adapter (CGA) and Enhanced Graphics Adapter (EGA) monitors, both of which have lower resolution and quality.

40. My monitor is making a clicking noise. It flashes sometimes. Is this all right?

Don't worry. This is just the computer and monitor getting synchronized.

More definitions:

Analog monitor: A monitor that can display an infinite range of colors.

Digital monitor: A monitor that can only show shades of gray or a limited number of colors.

Pixel: The smallest image displayable by a printer or monitor. In most monitors, each pixel is a combination of red, green, and blue. The term comes from PICTure ELement.

Super Video Graphics Array (SVGA): A monitor that is better than a standard VGA monitor. If enough video memory is available, an SVGA can display over 15 million colors. SVGA resolution is also superior; it can run from 800 by 600 pixels up to 1,024 by 1,280 pixels.

PRINTERS

Many problems can occur with printers. We will examine:

1. General problems with laser printers.

2. Problems as seen on printed pages.

3. Problems with dot matrix and bubble-jet (inkjet) printers.

You can of course solve many problems by going to the manufacturer's web site; these sites often provide troubleshooting information on error codes, etc. And other general rules need to be known:

- Before assuming a worst-case scenario, always try turning the printer on and off to clear offending data, turning the computer on and off for the same reason, and checking all connections.

- Remember to have the computer running before activating the printer. Also, get a cover for the printer to keep dust out. Store any components (such as cartridges for bubble-jet printers and ribbons for dot-matrix printers) in a cool dry place out of the light or in a special ink storage container.

- Read all instructions carefully, especially those for replacing cartridges and drums.

Laser Printers

41. My printer won't turn on. What can I do?

- Many printers have fuses. Check them; have spare fuses handy at all times.

- Check that power is reaching the printer. Sometimes a power outage can knock out your power strip and your equipment.

- Make sure that all indicator lights are functioning.

- Plug the printer into another outlet in case the outlet is faulty.

42. My printer is on but won't initialize. What can I do?

- One or more of the printer cartridges may not be properly installed. Someone may have installed the cartridges without removing the tape or holding adhesive.

- Check for an error condition indicated on the LCD or LED readout on the panel of the printer.

- If you have a Mac computer that uses a Chooser and this does not appear in the Apple menu, your system file may be old or you might not be properly connected to the printer. Or, perhaps you instructed the computer to delete this file.

43. My printer is on and has initialized, but it won't print anything I send it. What can I do?

- Check that all cables are tight and all connections are in good shape.

- Make sure the printer is set for On-line and not Off-line (some computers call this Ready/In Use or Not Ready/Not in Use).

- Close the top cover (and any inside covers) printer.

- Make sure the cartridges are all seated properly.

- See if the cartridges still have sealing tape on them (as when you first get them from the manufacturer); if so, remove it.

- Make sure enough paper is in the paper feeder; some printers will not print with only one or two sheets.

- See if there may be too much paper in the paper feeder; this may have caused a jam or misfeed. The wrong weight of paper can also cause these problems. With some printers, it's possible to put the paper in the wrong way; check the alignment.

- Allow plenty of time for the computer to send and the printer to process the file, especially if it's large or complex (with graphics, etc.).

- Check for error messages displayed by the printer.

- Print a self-test page to see whether the computer is talking to itself (many printers require you to go off-line to do this). If so, go to the next question.

- If you have booted the computer while the printer is on, you may have caused a communication error. Turn the computer and printer off, and then turn the computer on first and the printer second.

- Check that Spooling has been enabled. To do this:

    1. Click on the Start button, Settings, and then Printers.

    2. Double-click on the printer icon (or right-click on the printer icon and select Properties).

    3. Click on Properties from the Printer drop-down menu.

    4. Click on the Details tab.

    5. Inside this dialog box, click on Spool Settings.

    6. Click on the button that indicates the following action: Spool print jobs so program finished printing faster.

CAUTION: If you're computer-savvy, check the Autoexec.bat and the Config.sys files to see if there is a conflict. DO NOT TOUCH these files if you don't know what you're doing.

Definitions:

Autoexec.bat: In Microsoft's disk operating system (MS-DOS), the abbreviated format for the AUTOmatically EXECuted BATch file. This file saves the computer from having to enter frequently used commands, especially for sequential or repetitious operations.

Config.sys: In Microsoft's disk operating system (MS-DOS), an American Standard Code for Information Interchange (ASCII) text file in the root or parent directory containing configuration commands. This file is necessary for system startup.

44. My printer is on, has initialized, and can print its self-test page, but it won't print anything. What can I do?

- The interface between the computer and the printer may be defective. Go through all the steps listed in questions 41 through 43.

- Your system may not recognize your printer. To see if it does, do the following:

1. Click on the Start button, Settings, and then Printers.

2. If you see an icon for your printer, your system probably recognizes it.

3. If not, go to question 46 below, which discusses how to add a printer.

- You may need to set your printer as the default printer. To do this:

  1. Click on the Start button, Settings, and then Printers.

  2. Double-click on your printer icon (or right-click on the printer icon and select Set as Default).

  3. Click on Set as Default from the Printer drop-down menu.

  4. Or you can open any of your software packages and press Ctrl+P. When the Print window appears, it will list which printer is selected as the default printer.

45. My printer doesn't seem to be printing. The cables are connected, etc. What else could be the problem?

- Check what port the printer is connected to by doing the following:

  1. Click on Start, Settings, Control Panel, and then Printers.

  2. Double-click on your printer (or right-click and select Properties).

  3. Select Properties from one of the drop-down menus (usually Printer).

  4. Select the Details tab or the one showing port selection.[1]

---

[1]You can get to the same dialog box by going to Start, Settings, Printers, and double-clicking on the printer icon (or right-clicking and selecting Properties). Select Properties and then Details as before.

- Another way to check ports is to:

  1. Click on Start, Settings, and then Control Panel.

  2. Click on the System icon.

  3. Click on the + symbol to the left of Ports.

  4. Below that, click on highlight Printer Port.

  5. Click on the Properties button below (or you can right-click the Printer Port and select Properties).

  6. Inside this dialog box, you will probably see the General, Driver, and Resources tabs.

  General: Indicates the device is working.

  Driver: Shows whether a driver exists or is needed. You can add any needed driver here if you have the file on a CD-ROM or a floppy disk; many up-to-date drivers can be downloaded from the manufacturer's Internet web site.

  Resources: Shows which Interrupt ReQuest (IRQ) has been reserved for the printer and if a there is a conflict—which may happen, for instance, if you just installed a new device (say a tape drive) that has been trying to use the same IRQ as the printer. If so, try re-installing the new device. (For Windows 3.X, you may have to reload the unidriv.dll file, which is more complicated than can be discussed here.)

Definitions:

Device Driver (also called Driver): A software program that allows the hardware peripherals to talk to the computer. This program tells the peripheral (say a mouse or the keyboard) what your instructions mean (for instance, when typing the letter A or moving the mouse and clicking).

Interrupt ReQuest (IRQ): A communication route carrying signals to tell the brain of the computer to stop what it is doing and wait for further instructions. Each device has its own IRQ; there is a hierarchy in which the higher numbers get priority: A hard drive may have IRQ14 and the mouse may have IRQ12, meaning the hard drive is taken care of first.

Virtual Device Driver (VxD or vxd): This mimics buffers between your hardware and software. With so much information flying around in the computer at lightning speed, the VxD ensures that the right data reaches the right software (ever thought about how an Excel file knows to go to the Excel program?). Occasionally, you will see other designations, such as VmD. The middle letter indicates the type of hardware ("m" for mouse, in this case).

46. I don't see my printer icon. How do I add my printer?

If you don't see your printer as a selection in the Printers area, go to the Add Printer Wizard:

1. Have your CD-ROM or floppy disk with the printer information/file ready.

2. Click on Start, Settings, and then Printers.

3. Double-click on the Add Printer icon.

4. Click on Next to move to the next step after you make your choice for each of the boxes in the following steps.

5. Choose your printer as local (unless you're connected to a network).

6. In the next box, select the manufacturer (on the left-hand side) and the specific computer (on the right-hand side).

7. Choose your printer port. (You will probably only have one possibility, or the computer will have already chosen it for you.)

8. Choose the name of the printer. Use what the computer gives you; do not rename the printer for now.

9. The Add Printer Wizard will ask if you want to print a test page. Select Yes to see if your new selection is working.

10. Turn off (not just restart) the computer and printer completely.

11. Turn both back on and try to print a document to make sure everything is working.

47. My printer seems to be printing, but the pages are blank. What can I do?

• Check if a "Low Toner" indicator is flashing or these words appear on the LCD or LED screen for the computer in case your toner cartridge is empty.

• Some printers have a print density dial inside them. Check your printer manual if you have one and its location. If you have one, adjust it.

• Check the printer properties to see that the default selections allow for a dark enough print:

1. Click on Start, Settings, and then Printers.

2. Double-click on your printer.

3. Select Properties from the drop-down menu; select the tab (usually called Graphics) that deals with paper and adjust accordingly.

• The printer and the computer may have different values for how many lines they accept per page as normal. For instance, you could be printing a resume, which has an additional blank line (which you do not at first notice); the extra carriage return is printing the second page, which is naturally blank.

• The document you are sending is in a format your printer will not understand. For instance, if your computer is configured for PostScript (PS) and you send a Hewlett-Packard (HP) formatted document, the printer will print garbled text. Some printers can switch back and forth; many cannot.

Definitions:

PostScript (PS) font: A type of lettering format (font) employed by Adobe Systems. A PostScript printer, for instance, will automatically use PostScript instead of other fonts available, such as bit-mapped font.

Printed Pages

Check your manual's troubleshooting section (always a good idea anyway), since each printer or computer has its own peculiar characteristics and solutions. If you have no manual, call the manufacturer, the store where you bought the printer, or the manufacturer's web site.

48. The pages are coming out black or way too dark. What can I do?

- Sometimes, pages will look black when you install a new drum or cartridge. Print a few more pages to see if the problem takes care of itself.

- A defective toner cartridge may be the culprit. If you have a spare toner cartridge, replace the first cartridge to see if the problem disappears.

- If the pages are coming out pure black, the toner cartridge is probably defective.

- A charge wire could be broken. You will have to take the printer to a repair shop.

- In Apple printers, adjust the print density dial.

49. The pages have a vertical streak. What can I do?

- A consistent vertical streak can mean a scratch on the drum; you must buy a new drum. (This is a major reason why manufacturers instruct you never ever touch the surface of the drum. Even a thumbprint can ruin your pages.

- A vertical streak can also indicate a hardware problem. Reinstall your printer software, check with the manufacturer for updated drivers, etc.

50. The pages have streaks or waves. What can I do?

- There may be dirt inside the printer area or the toner may be low. Keep everything clean (spotless, in fact); use the type of cleaning solution recommended by the manufacturer. Use a can of compressed air and blow out the area carefully.

- Try shaking the toner cartridge horizontally to distribute the toner evenly. (First, make sure the cartridge windows are closed.)

- In Apple printers, a dirty corona wire, transfer guide, or discharging pins could be causing the streaks; clean them. You may also need to shake or replace the toner cartridge.

51. I see repeating marks on my pages. What can I do?

- The drum may be defective. You will have to replace it. Consult your manufacturer's guide on how to do this.

- The roller may be dirty. Clean them with a solution recommended by the manufacturer.

- The fuser roller may be dirty. Consult your manufacturer's guide to determine how to remove and replace the roller.

52. My pages have white lines. What can I do?

- The cartridge may be blocked. If you look at cartridges, you may see blades ("doctor blades"). Their job is to clean away excess toner; occasionally, they become clogged, preventing toner from reaching the page. Use a can of compressed air to carefully remove excess toner.

- Try holding and shaking the toner cartridge horizontally to distribute the toner evenly. (First, make sure the cartridge windows are closed.)

53. The printing quality is uneven. What can I do?

- Take the cartridge out of the printer and shake it back and forth horizontally to redistribute the toner. (Before shaking, make sure the cartridge windows are closed.) If the toner is low, shaking the cartridge can increase the life of the cartridge.

- If the printer has a photoreceptor and light is somehow hitting it, the exposure will be thrown off—much like a flash ruining part of a photograph. Consult your manufacturer's guide for the location of the photoreceptor to determine if light is striking it. If light is hitting the photoreceptor, move the printer away from the light source. If this does not alleviate the problem, contact the manufacturer.

Definitions:

Photoreceptor: An electronic eye that registers the amount of incoming light.

54. My pages have no gray tones. What can I do?

- Black and white tones only with no gray tones on the page could indicate an incorrect driver. Do the following:

  1. Have ready the CD-ROMs or floppy disks that have the files needed for this procedure.

  2. Click on Start, Settings, and then Control Panel.

  3. Double-click on the System icon.

  4. Click on the Device Manager tab.

  5. Click on the + sign next to Ports (COM & LPT).

  6. Click on Printer Port (LPT1). This line will be highlighted.

  7. Click on the Properties button.

  8. Click on the Driver tab. Here you will be able to see whether your computer needs a driver. If the Driver tab window indicates you need a driver, click on Update Driver and follow the directions.

9. For Apple printers, ensure the grayscale is activated from the Color/Grayscale button in the Print dialog box.

55. The characters on the page are gobbledygook. What can I do?

• This is usually a setup problem. For instance, you want to use PostScript fonts and the printer has been set up for Hewlett-Packard (HP) emulation mode. Change the emulation mode; consult the printer manufacturer's documentation for the proper procedure.

• You could have the wrong font set checked; for instance, the Wingdings font type could look garbled when you print it.

• Make sure the printer cable is connected tightly enough.

• Check the font selected for the software you're using:

• Click on Start, Settings, and then Printers.

  1. Double-click on the printer icon (or right-click on the printer icon and select Properties).

  2. Click on Properties from the drop-down menu.

  3. Click on the Fonts tab. Here, you will have several buttons to choose from, which vary with each operating system, but they're self-explanatory.

56. The images and graphics are coming out garbled or not at all. What can I do?

• Check to see if you have enough memory for the printer. To see how much memory is currently selected:

  1. Click on Start, Settings, and Printers.

  2. Double-click on the printer icon (or right-click on the printer icon and select Properties).

  3. Click on Properties from the drop-down menu.

4. Click on the Device Options tab (or the tab showing memory in your computer). You will have to reduce the size of the file or increase the amount of memory. If you choose to increase memory, contact your manufacturer to learn about adding memory cards.

57. The paper is wrinkling (or the labels are curling). What can I do?

- This is usually the result of an improperly maintained printer, paper that is too light or heavy (20-pound weight is the norm), or worn rollers or feeders.

- Wrinkled pages can also result from trying to feed envelopes into a printer not designed for this task.

- The labels may have come unglued from their backing sheet, especially if they are old.

58. The paper is jamming. What can I do?

- Paper jams can be caused by the same problem as wrinkled pages.

- Many people like to turn a page over and reuse it. Reused paper sometimes jams, sometimes slips by without being used, and sometimes works.

- Paper jams can result from worn parts like feeders, rollers, sensors, or gears.

- Try fanning the paper before you put it in the tray; this increases separation of the pages and makes it easier for the printer to grab each page.

- The paper may have too much cotton content with threads causing jamming.

- There may be too much paper in the tray.

- The paper may be too smooth, too moist, or too dry.

- Check whether you have the right paper size for printing:

    1. Click on Start, Settings, and then Printers.

    2. Double-click on your printer icon (or right-click on the printer icon and select Properties).

    3. Click on Properties from the drop-down menu

    4. Click on the Paper tab. You can change paper types within each software program.

- In Hewlett-Packard (HP) printers, the most common error message for jamming is Error 41.3 (now you know what that number means).

59. My printer is printing, but the page on the screen doesn't match the printed page. What can I do?

- Check the margin settings for your printer and within the software. For instance, you may want to print Portrait, yet you may have the printer set for Landscape, or vice versa. Improper margins could also throw off graphics, which could still look fine on the screen. To check margins for the entire computer:

    1. Click on Start, Settings, and then Printers.

    2. Double-click on your printer icon (or right-click on the printer icon and select Properties).

    3. Click on Properties from the drop-down menu.

    4. Click on the Paper tab.

- Within a particular software package, check the Print Preview (or similar function) that can give you a What-You-See-Is-What-You-Get (WYSIWYG) view.

Dot-matrix Printers

Dot-matrix printers come in two flavors: 9-pin (lower resolution) and 24-pin (higher resolution). The main logic board controls how the pins interact with one another to produce letters and images on the page. (Even though laser printers are more complicated, you would do well to upgrade to them; laser printer prices have dropped dramatically over the years, the quality is higher, and they are quieter than dot-matrix printers.)

The main reason dot-matrix printers have fallen out of favor is their quality cannot match that of laser printers because of technological limitations. The only advantage is that a dot-matrix printer can accept a heavier weight paper or multiple-layer paper such as a form in triplicate.

As usual with hardware problems, don't forget to check the cables and then restart the printer and computer. As always, consult your manual, the manufacturer, technicians at your place of purchase, and web sites.

60. My printed pages are coming out too light. What can I do?

- The ribbon has become dry or run out of ink (just as in a standard typewriter). Install a new one.

- The pins are clogged with ink.

  1. Turn off the printer.

  2. Use a can of compressed air and carefully blow the ink out if possible.

  3. Use a cotton swab dipped in an alcohol-based cleaner and lightly clean the clogged ink area.

61. The carriage is moving back and forth but nothing is printing. What can I do?

- Check that the ribbon is correctly installed.

- Check to see if a pressure, or gap, lever exists (for how dark you want the image/text); if so, make sure it's set dark enough.

62. The carriage has stopped moving and all the indicator lights are blinking like crazy. What can I do?

- Some object like a torn piece of paper has probably blocked the print head. Do the following:

  1. Turn the power off.

  2. Check the print path. Any paper or pieces of paper jammed?

  3. Move the print head a little back and forth to see if it can move.

  4. Turn the printer back on.

- Other (more serious) possibilities are bad motors, bad gears, broken belts, or a software problem.

Definitions:

Print head: The mechanism within the printer that transfers letters and images to the paper. A dot-matrix printer has pins that strike the page through an inked ribbon; inkjet printers fire color out from the print head. Laser printers do not have print heads; they work more like a photocopier.

63. The printing is faint. What can I do?

- The pressure, or gap lever, is probably set too light. Consult your manual to find out where this lever is. It's usually this printer to the left or right (and in front) of the carriage mechanism.

64. My printer is smearing the ink. What can I do?

- Check the pressure, or gap lever, for proper adjustment.

65. The printer is working, but the characters are weird. What can I do?

- Check to make sure you have the correct emulation mode. You will probably have to take the printer off-line (look on the LCD or LED readout of the printer panel) and then follow your manufacturer's documentation to find out which emulation you have.

66. The printer is working but is vertically double-spacing all the text. What can I do?

- Most dot matrix printers have an AUTO LF function (AUTO LF means Automatic Line Feed.) If AUTO LF is on, it will add a blank line every time it senses a carriage return. Turn the LF off, and the double spacing should go away. Usually, you turn this off anyway because the computer is already sending the LF command as part of the software.

67. The printer is working but is printing all the text on one line. What can I do?

- This problem is the opposite found in question 66. The AUTO LF function in the printer is off, but the computer is not sending any LF signal that the printer recognizes. Either turn on the printer AUTO LF, or fix the carriage return problem in the software you're currently using. For instance, in Word, click on the Format drop-down menu and then Paragraph; select Double spacing from the Line spacing box.

Bubble-jet (Inkjet) Printers

Since most inkjet printers use color, you can have problems with print head alignment, resolution, and more that may cause inks to bleed. Some say you should consider color laser printers, but they are costly to buy and maintain and the bubble-jets do as good a job.

Begin by checking cables and restarting the printer and computer. As always, consult your manual, manufacturer, place of purchase, and web sites.

68. Can you give me some general information about these printers?

- Most inkjet printer problems can be prevented with proper cleaning and lubrication. Check the manufacturer's web site for maintenance techniques and other tips.

- It's important that you shut off the printer using its own switch, not from a surge protector or other external power source. The print head is parked in a special spot to prevent the nozzles from drying out. If you turn off the printer from the surge protector, the print head may not reach its "parking spot"; it will then dry out, causing all sorts of printing problems.

69. My pages are coming out blank. What can I do?

- Chances are you have a dry cartridge or a cartridge with a dried and clogged carriage. To try to save it:

  1. Move the cartridge to its removal position in the printer

  2. Remove the cartridge.

  3. Unplug the printer. Do not touch the ink jet areas or the electrical contacts. Do not wipe the nozzle plate. Do not use alcohol-based cleaners; instead, check your manual. In fact, when you are not using the cartridges, put them in specially designed storage boxes.

  4. Set the cartridge in a shallow pool of ink for several hours. If this doesn't help, you will probably have to buy a new cartridge.

70. My printer is printing horizontal lines. What can I do?

- Try cleaning the ink cartridge carriage:

  1. Most cartridges have a removal position in the printer. Remove the cartridge after it reaches this point.

  2. Unplug the printer. Do not touch the ink jet areas or the electrical contacts. Do not wipe the nozzle plate. Do not use alcohol-based cleaners; instead, check your manual. In fact, when you are not using the cartridges, place them in specifically designed storage boxes. These will prevent the nozzles from becoming clogged.

3. Follow the manufacturer's instructions for cleaning the cartridge.

71. My prints are coming out faded. What can I do?

• Try cleaning the jet plate area or the contact strip with a damp towel to get rid of paper dust.

72. The color of my prints doesn't seem right. What can I do?

• Check in your manual how to do a proper purge, especially of the black ink.

73. My printer is making too much noise. Is this noise acceptable?

• Chances are the printer has a dirty guide rail. Check your printer manual as to what type of cleaner and oil to use.

STORAGE DEVICES

Hard Drives

Hard drives are the basis of most computers. You need a hard drive to store your operating system, applications, and files, but few people understand them. This section is designed to help you understand how a hard drive works.

74. I have a two-gigabyte (2 GB) hard disk and I only have 1.5 GB of programs installed, but I keep getting "Disk Full" error messages. What's wrong?

• When you delete a file from Windows 95, it doesn't get removed from the hard drive. Instead, it gets copied into the directory called Recycle Bin. To get rid of the files completely and release space on the hard drive, you must delete the files from the Recycle Bin icon on the desktop. To do that:

1. Double-click on the Recycle Bin icon on your desktop.

2. Click on one of the listed files.

3. Press Ctrl + A (which selects all of the listed files), or and delete.

4. Right click on the File drop-down menu.

5. Click on Empty Recycle Bin.

6. Click on OK.

CAUTION: Make sure you're not unintentionally erasing any files you would like to keep. Once you delete a file from the Recycle Bin, it's usually gone forever. However, if you're working in Windows NT, you may have another chance to get the file back.

• Another possibility is that most browsers (like Netscape and Microsoft Internet Explorer) have a Cache directory located within their program folders. This directory is where all web pages are stored while browsing the Internet. The cache accelerates loading of web pages. If you visit a web page, the location and file are cached. When you leave this web site and return, the page doesn't have to be downloaded from the server again; it can be recalled from the Cache directory on your hard drive. If you haven't set a limit on the size of the Cache directory, it will fill up with these files and eat up all the space on the hard drive.

Your software should let you purge the cache:

1. Open, say, Netscape (you don't have to be connected to the Internet).

2. Click on the Edit drop-down menu, and then Preferences. (Or press Alt+E, E.)

3. Click on Navigator (double-clicking on Navigator will bring you choices for Smart Browsing, etc., which will be discussed later).

4. Go to the History section to the right and below. Type 0 (zero) if you want the web pages cleaned as soon as you leave and close Netscape.

5. To do your own housecleaning, click on the Clear History button.

6. To do more housecleaning, click on the Clear Location Bar button.

7. Click on OK.

Another way exists to clean the cache files:

1. Open Netscape (you don't have to be connected to the Internet).

2. Click on the Edit drop-down menu, and then Preferences. (Or, press Alt+E, E.)

3. Double-click on Advanced.

4. Click on Cache.

5. Click on Clear Memory Cache button and click on OK.

6. Click on Clear Disk Cache button and click on OK.

7. In the Memory Cache and Disk Cache boxes, increase the number in the textbox. I had enough storage space to type in 65536 (or some multiple of two). The larger the number the more site can be cached.

- Print Manager offers you a third option (this is installed by default). A file that is printed is saved on the hard disk until it can be sent to the printer. A large graphic or image can take up a lot of disk space. If this is a problem for you, delete any unneeded files or applications from your hard drive.

- A fourth option is available only for large drives. Setting the drive up as a single large drive (or partition) results in a lot of wasted space when your computer saves files because the method normally used to partition a drive (that is, to make it ready to be used by dividing it into sections) defines the minimum amount of space a file can take. The larger the partition, the larger the minimum size.

When you format a drive, many spaces or blocks on the drive contain storage space for files and applications. This space is called a cluster.

Many drives are formatted into 32 kilobyte (32KB) clusters, so that, in the case of a two-gigabyte drive, every file will take up at least 32KB of disk space, even one only 10KB in size. If you have a lot of little files, a lot of space is wasted because if the files may be taking up space they don't need.

To make matters worse, 32KB is the minimum cluster size. A file too big for one cluster will take up all of two, so a 33KB file will absorb 64KB of storage space. Of course, if your files are large, the space wasted becomes smaller—but the average system has more small files than large ones.

If you are using Windows 95 B or newer, the cluster size will be only 4KB, not 32KB. To check which version of Windows you have, do the following:

1. Right-click on the My Computer icon.

2. Click on Properties. This opens the System Properties dialog box.

3. Click on the General tab. At the top of the window you will see System, then Microsoft Windows 95 or 98. Below that should read something like "4.00 950 B." As long as there is a letter "B" at the end, you have Windows 95 B or newer.

Definitions:

Cache: A temporary storage area on the hard drive for frequently used information. Used by web browsers, the operating system, and system memory.

Cache Directory: Folder in Netscape and Internet Explorer that holds previously viewed web pages.

Cluster: When a drive is formatted, the spaces or blocks on the drive that contain storage space for files and applications.

75. Why does the data from my old, smaller hard drive take up more space on my new, larger hard drive?

This is a limitation of the Windows operating system, not your hard drive. When you formatted the drive (whether with the utility that came with the drive or one from a different source), you had several options. The most common method is to create one large partition. That can work fine, but as hard drives get larger, a single partition can limit the usable space on the drive. You need to decide whether or not to partition the drive at 100 percent or to split the drive into extended and logical drives.

Which option is best for you? Check out the following example:

- If you run programs that create a lot of small files, partition the drive for a smaller size.

- If you run programs that create a few very large files, a single large partition should work fine.

- If you're not sure which option is best for you, we recommend one large partition.

CAUTION: Formatting a drive will completely erase its contents. Be sure to back up all your data and applications before proceeding.

76. My hard disk was sold to me as a 3.2GB drive, but I only show a formatted capacity of 3.05GB. Was I actually sold a smaller drive?

Most operating systems report the capacity of the hard drive using the assumption that one megabyte (1MB) is equal to 1,048,576 bytes. Technically, this is correct.

Hardware manufacturers consider 1MB to be equal to 1,000,000 bytes. You can see where this can cause confusion! If the drive is advertised as 3.2 gigabytes or 3.2 GB (3,200,000,000 bytes), the operating system will see it as approximately 3.05GB (3,200,000,000/ 1,048,576 / 1000 = 3.051758125). The full 3,200,000,000 bytes are there; the amounts are presented differently.

This mathematical confusion can occur for drives of any size. If you are being that careful about every byte of memory, you might want to get a larger drive so you don't have to worry about running out of drive space. Everyone should have at least 50 to 100 MB of space available at all times.

77. Are bad sectors supposed to be on the drive?

No. All modern drives support error management, which hides bad sectors that may be on the disk before leaving the factory. Even a single bad sector is sufficient grounds to return the drive under warranty. If you want to continue using a computer with a bad sector on the hard drive, prepare yourself for lost data and system crashes.

Definitions:

Sector: Storage area of a hard drive. Typically, a sector is a segment of a concentric track encoded on a floppy disk or hard disk in a low-level format; it usual contains 512 bytes of information.

78. Help! Windows 95 and Windows 98 indicate my drive uses compatibility mode! What does this mean?

It usually means you have a virus. Get an anti-virus program; they're sold by Norton and McAfee, among others.

WARNING: Viruses on your hard drive can affect all files. To avoid spreading the virus, do not send files via e-mail or on disk to anyone else.

Definitions:

Virus: A piece of software designed to infect a computer and or its peripherals. Like many biological viruses, a software virus embeds itself inside the host program; it may be activated immediately or stay dormant for a while. Viruses on a floppy disk are often called boot viruses.

Viruses *cannot* attach themselves or be attached to data. They must hitchhike with a program, very often an executable program. Once you activate the program, you start the virus. Besides boot viruses, there are macro viruses, worms, stealth viruses, and more.

79. Windows 95 sees my partitions, but DOS does not. What's wrong?

An error may have occurred if you have used a utility like Fdisk (in Windows 95) to partition your drive. It can happen because Windows 95 can't recognize drives larger than eight gigabytes (8GB). To avoid the problem, partitions that extend beyond 8GB must be made invisible. Unfortunately, Fdisk sometimes hides partitions this way even if your drive is much smaller than 8GB. Fdisk also hides them from all other operating systems, including older versions of DOS, which can cause all kinds of problems.

To get to the Fdisk application:

1. Close all other applications.

2. Make sure you've backed up ALL important files.

3. Go to Windows Explorer.

4. Double-click on the Windows (or Windows.000) folder for your hard drive (the letter designation is usually C).

5. Double-click on the Command folder.

6. Double-click on the Fdisk icon on the right.

7. Follow instructions within the DOS screen.

CAUTION: Only use Fdisk if you know what you are doing. Otherwise, you can lose all the information and applications on your hard drive. If you're not sure how to use the Fdisk application, *don't use it*. Consult an expert to assist you.

Under certain circumstances, these new partition types can completely mess things up when you're going from the Windows 95 graphical shell to MS-DOS mode. Drive contents may appear to be corrupted or be replaced by the contents of the hard drive. Don't try anything fancy when this happens; you can easily corrupt your data at this stage. Don't use the "Restart in MS-DOS mode" option, and don't run programs configured to run in MS-DOS mode. MS-DOS *windows* are still fine.

The most comfortable way to fix this is to change the partition types using a program called Partition Magic—but *ONLY* version 2.03 or higher. You can get an update patch for older versions or contact your software distributor for availability.

The alternative is to back up your data and repartition the drive using the program FDISK/X, which disables the new partition types, or use DOS 6 FDISK. Be sure to apply any other Windows 95 bugfixer that is available from Microsoft's web site at *http://www.microsoft.com.*

Definitions:

Fdisk (or FDISK/X): A program that allows you to partition a hard drive.

80. I've heard of programs that can compress my hard drive so that it can hold more files. Is there any risk in using these programs?

Yes. Used improperly, these programs can compress important system files, making your computer unusable. Given that these programs cost about almost as much as a new hard drive, but offer more risk and less drive space, the better alternative is to use the money to buy a new, larger hard drive. One such program you should *not* use is DriveSpace, even though it comes with the Windows 95 operating system. It may create some of the problems explained above.

Definitions:

Basic Input/Output System (BIOS): Software coded into computer chips for various purposes. The BIOS on the motherboard of Windows-based computers is the program used to boot and control the computer.

File Allocation Table (FAT): Determines the block size in Windows and keeps track of where data are stored on the disks. Fat16 is a 16KB block found on the first version of Windows 95. Fat 32 superseded FAT16; it's a 4KB Block found on all Windows 95 and Windows 98. FAT32 can support hard drives up to two terabytes (2TB).

CD-ROM Drives

Though CD-ROM drives have been standard on computers for almost a decade, there are many variations of speed types and interfaces.

Until recently, not much has changed with them except faster drives. Now, the digital versatile disk (DVD) is becoming the standard in computers as well as in home entertainment. We'll talk about DVD later in the chapter, but first look at the regular CD-ROM drives on the market.

Definitions:

Compact Disk-Read Only Memory (CD-ROM): A compact disk read-only optical storage technology. CD-ROM disks are often used for encyclopedias and software libraries. Compression techniques make it possible to store 650 MB or 250,000 text pages on one CD-ROM disk. A CD-ROM can hold text, video imagery, audio, or graphics.

Digital Versatile Disk (DVD): (Originally called digital video disk). A high-capacity optical disk used to store everything from massive computer applications to full-length movies. While similar in physical size and appearance to a CD-ROM, DVD is a huge leap of technology: A standard single-layer single-sided DVD can store 4.7 GB of data; the two-layer standard increases capacity to 8.5GB and the double-sided two-layer standard has a maximum storage capacity of 17GB. To use DVDs, you'll probably need a new drive, but they can read your older CD-ROMs and audio CDs.

NOTE: The spelling "disk" is usually used for floppy disks or for the disk operating system. The spelling "disc" is used for hard disc drives, CDs, and DVDs.

81. I installed a new hard drive and now my CD-ROM drive has a different drive letter. This is causing all kinds of problems with programs that use the CD-ROM, including the music CDs. What's going on here?

The disk operating system (DOS) first assigns drive letters to hard drives, then to the CD-ROM. Even though Microsoft doesn't advertise it, DOS is part of Windows 95 and 98. You cannot assign the CD-ROM a drive letter lower than the last hard disk letter. However, you can assign a specific drive letter (beyond the DOS drives) to your CD-ROM. To do this:

1. Click on the Start button, Settings, Control Panel, and then the System icon.

2. Click on the Device Manager tab.

3. Double-click on CD-ROM.

4. Double-click on the CD-ROM shown.

5. Click on the Settings tab.

6. Under Reserved Drive Letters, click on the drop-down arrow to set the CD-ROM drive letter to be the same for Start Drive Letter and End Drive Letter.

7. Click on the OK button.

NOTE: The end drive letter may be different if you have more than one CD-ROM installed or if you have a multi-CD player.

Definitions:

Disk Operating System (DOS): A Microsoft operating system (control program) for personal computers, especially for Windows 3.1. A modified version of DOS is included with Windows 95 and Windows 98.

82. Why did my CD-ROM suddenly stop working?

• Viruses could be the culprits. A lot of them will attack a CD-ROM and cause the drive to vanish from your desktop. As always, try turning the computer off, checking cable connections, et cetera, as a first line of defense. Run a virus protection program like Norton Antivirus or McAfee.

- If there are no viruses, check the device manager control panel:

  1. Click on the Start button, Settings, Control Panel, and then the System icon.

  2. Click on the Device Manager tab.

  3. Double-click on CD-ROM.

  4. Check if your computer is showing a CD-ROM.

- If it doesn't show up there could be a problem with the CD disk, the drive itself, the controller, or the cable. To check some these possible problems:

  1. Turn the computer and monitor off.

  2. Disconnect the power cable to your computer.

  3. Take the cover off your computer. (A Phillips screwdriver is probably all you need to do this.)

  4. Unplug the drive cable.

  5. Plug it back in at both the drive connection and motherboard ends.

  6. Screw the computer cover back on.

  7. Connect all cables.

  8. Turn the computer and monitor back on.

  9. Check the device manager control panel (the same four steps immediately above these). If the CD-ROM doesn't appear after you check cables and reboot the computer, something may be broken in the CD-ROM drive. Call the manufacturer for assistance or contact the store where you bought the computer.

- If the CD-ROM is detected but DOS or Windows doesn't see it, you may have a driver issue. Make sure that the appropriate drivers are installed. Usually, Windows 95 is looking for a 32-bit protected-mode driver (called vcdfsd.vxd or cdvsd.vxd) or some variation. It's also a good idea to check the drive manufacturer's web site for the latest drivers. To check you have drivers for the CD-ROM:

1. Be sure you have ready the appropriate Windows 95 or Windows 98 disk to load the driver.

2. Click on the Start button, Settings, Control Panel, and then the System icon.

3. Click on the Device Manager tab.

4. Double-click on CD-ROM.

5. Double-click on the CD-ROM shown.

6. Click on the Driver tab.

7. If no driver appears and one is needed, click on the Update Driver button and follow the instructions.

NOTE: If this procedure doesn't solve the problem, you may want to contact the manufacturer (via phone, e-mail, or their web site) to see if you need a different driver.

Definitions:

Device Driver (also called a Driver): A software program that allows hardware peripherals to talk to the computer. It tells the peripheral (mouse, keyboard, CD-ROM) what your instructions mean (for instance, when typing the letter A or moving the mouse and clicking).

Motherboard: Also called the logic board. Part of every computer system, the largest printed circuit board in your computer. It usually contains the central processing unit (CPU) chip, the controller circuitry, the bus, and sockets for additional boards called daughtercards.

Virus: A piece of software designed to infect a computer or its peripherals. Like many biological viruses, a software virus embeds itself inside the host program; it can be activated immediately or may wait till a later time. Viruses inside a floppy disk are often called boot viruses. Viruses cannot attach themselves or be attached to data. They must hitchhike with a program, often an executable program. Once you activate the program, you launch the virus. Other types of viruses are macro viruses, worms, and stealth viruses.

83. How do I get the CD-ROM active under Safe Mode?

To activate the CD-ROM:

1. Turn on the computer, monitor, and any other appropriate devices.

2. Press the F8 button on your keyboard as soon as "Starting Windows 95/98" or "OS Load In Progress" appears.

3. Select Command Prompt Only from the Microsoft Windows 95/98 Startup Menu.

4. At the C: prompt type WIN /D:M. Once Safe Mode loads, the CD-ROM will be active.

If you want to know more about Windows, check out Windows 95 Secrets (4th ed., 1997: IDG Books) by Brian Livingston and Davis Straub, *Windows 98 Secrets* (1998: IDG Books) by Brian Livingston and Davis Straub, or *Windows 2000 Secrets* (2000: IDG Books) by Brian Livingston, Bruce Brown, and Bruce Kratofil.

If you want to learn more about Safe Mode, here are some additional commands you can run. Only use these commands if you feel technically capable. Otherwise, ask an expert, manufacturer, computer store personnel, or a web site technician for assistance.

WIN [/D:[M][N]

/D   = Used for troubleshooting when Windows doesn't start correctly.
[M]   = Enables Safe Mode. This is automatically enabled during Safe
        start (function key F5).
[N]   = Enables Safe Mode with networking; automatically enabled
        during Safe Mode start (function key F6).

Definitions:

Safe Mode: A method of troubleshooting Windows, especially when encountering conflicts. In Safe Mode, only the absolute minimum requirements (keyboard usage, etc.) are loaded. Only manipulate information in Safe Mode if you know what you're doing.

84. Why do some of my CDs work in my CD-ROM drive, while others don't?

*   Are they Mac or PC disks? Check the label. Most labels will show which operating systems the CD was designed to run under. Mac disks will not work on Windows CDs.

*   Your disk could be dirty. See question 85 for how to resolve this problem.

85. I had a CD that used to work in my drive, but now it doesn't work even though all my other disks do. What can I do?

Over time, disks tend to accumulate fingerprints, dust, and other forms of dirt. Clean the disk with a dry, soft cloth or buy a CD cleaning system. Don't use any cleaning solvents on the disks except those identified to work with CDs. You can find these products as your audio or computer store. If this doesn't work, check the answer to question 84.

TIP:

*   Always stores disks in their original container or a CD holder.

*   Never leave CDs lying around unprotected.

*   Never touch the bottom of the disk (the side without printing); your fingers and hands contain dirt and grease that can hinder the drive's laser reading of the CD data. Often, when you hear an audio CD start to repeat rapidly, the cause is a fingerprint.

*   Contrary to popular belief, CDs are destructible; they are easily scratched. A scratched CD-ROM may be unusable.

86. How do I test my CD-ROM drive to see if it's working?

To test whether your CD-ROM drive is functional:

1. Turn your computer, monitor, and peripherals off.

2. Unplug all power cables running to the computer.

3. Take the cover off your computer. (A Phillips screwdriver is probably all you need to do this.)

4. Remove the SCSI cable or IDE cable that connects the CD-ROM drive to the computer.

5. Replace the cover to the computer.

6. Plug all power cables back.

7. Turn your computer, monitor, and peripherals back on.

8. Insert an audio CD into the drive.

9. Press the left mouse button.

10. Plug in a set of headphones.

11. Can you hear music?

12. If you do, then it's working. If not, then contact the drive manufacturer for assistance in resolving the problem.

Definitions:

Enhanced Integrated Device Electronics (EIDE): (Also called Enhanced Integrated Drive Electronics). A standard built on the original IDE specifications. EIDE increases the previous maximum disk size from 504 MB to over 8 GB, more than doubles the data transfer rate over the original IDE specification, and doubles the number of drives a PC can contain to four.

Integrated Device Electronics (IDE): (Also called Integrated Drive Electronics). A hard-drive interface that has all the controller electronics integrated into the drive itself. The IDE specification handles hard disks up to 504 MB in size. Because of its simple instruction set and the short route between controller and drive, it is a quick and easy type of drive to use (unlike SCSI drives). But because it is a limited specification, IDE has been superseded by an enhanced version, EIDE.

Small Computer System Interface (SCSI) (pronounced scuzzy): A standard for hard drives, scanners, and CD-ROM drives. SCSI was first used on the Apple Macintosh. With SCSI, you can add up to seven new devices to your computer and allow them to deal with single-interface issues by themselves.

87. Why is my CD-ROM drive making noise?

The problem is due to the high rotation speeds in some drives; at around 12X speed or higher, unbalanced CDs may cause the CD-ROM drives to vibrate at a level that causes excessive noise. Disks with a lot of ink on one side of the disk, gold disks, colored compact disk recordable (CD-R) disks, or disks that have a label on one side can also cause this problem.

88. How can I turn off the Auto-Run feature on my CD-ROM?

It may be a good idea to turn off Auto-Run anyway; it could make your system a little faster since it will not have to check for a CD periodically. To turn off Auto-Run:

1. Click on the Start button, Settings, Control Panel, and then the System icon.

2. Click on the Device Manager tab.

3. Double-click the CD-ROM designation.

4. Click the available CD-ROM Drive.

5. Press the Properties button.

6. Select the Settings tab.

7. Uncheck Auto Insert Notification.

Just turning it off will not truly disable Auto-Run because another utility, Auto Insert Notification, is part of the CD's properties. Auto-Run, a property of Windows, and will run the file when the CD recognizes the Auto Insert Notification.

This means that even if you have Auto Insert Notification unchecked, Windows will still Auto-Run the CD when you double-click it. The only way to fix this is to get the free Microsoft utility PowerToys *(http://www.microsoft.com/windows95/downloads* under Power and Kernel Toys); you change it with the Tweak UI function. In this program, click the Paranoia tab and uncheck the play audio CD automatically option. This will ensure your CD does not Auto-Run.

Definitions:

PowerToys: A free utility from Microsoft that allows you to tweak the interface of Windows 95. PowerToys is available at *http://www. microsoft.com/windows95/downloads* under Power and Kernel Toys.

89. How do I install the Windows 95 disk without the CD-ROM key code on the CD case that it came on?

If you need to reinstall Windows 95, Windows 98, or any other Microsoft application from its CD-ROM, it calls for the CD key printed on the back of the CD-ROM sleeve. There may be times that this is not accessible because the disk is stored in a CD-caddy, the case may have broken and been thrown away, or any other reason that you can think of.

This is not a problem. When prompted by the computer during the install process, just enter any three characters, followed by a hyphen. Now enter 1111111 and select OK. Setup will proceed without a hitch. (Instead of 1111111, you can use any combination of seven numbers, which when added, equal a sum that is a multiple of seven, such as 1234567.)

NOTE: In no way do we suggest you use this tip to violate software licensing agreements. We only suggest this for people who have lost their key code.

90. Will my older CDs, with games, run on a faster CD-ROM drive?

Usually you will see a big difference switching from an older drive to a newer one. When playing games, the video will be smoother, and the sounds will play more evenly.

A CD application does not do anything until it is read off the CD and processed by the computer's CPU. With a faster drive, you spend less time waiting for the disk to be read. Also, if you're updating your computer, a newer chip will be process the data faster and also increase performance.

91. When playing games, my CD-ROM drive spins down after a few seconds of non-use. This delays the gaming action while it spins back up to full speed. How can I set it to full speed at all times?

The CD-ROM spins down to save energy. At this time, you cannot do anything to prevent it from spinning down.

92. Should I upgrade to a faster CD-ROM drive or get a DVD drive instead?

Because a DVD drive is the newest standard, it's your best investment. The costs of these drives have already fallen to price points near typical CD-ROM drives; most manufacturers are even including the DVD as the standard CD drive. DVD drives are backward compatible with all CD-ROM technology, and the transfer speeds were around 9X in the first-generation models. You get the added benefit of being able to access the new DVD entertainment and data titles that are available. With 4.7 GB per side, DVD-ROM will soon replace CD-ROM drives.

Definitions:

Basic Input/Output System (BIOS): Software coded into computer chips for various purposes. The BIOS on the motherboard of Windows-based computers is the program used to boot and control the computer.

Registry: The Windows Registry stores system configuration details, such as wallpaper, color schemes, and desktop arrangements, in a file called user.dat. It stores hardware and software-specific details, like device management and file extension information, in a file called system.dat. The registry in Windows 95 and later, replaces the functions of win.ini and system.ini files from earlier versions of Windows. Registry details can be edited using a program called RegEdit (which ships with Windows 95 and later) and exported to text format as a file with the extension REG.

Tape Drives

Tape drives have long been a mainstay for many computer users. They are a low-cost option to backup your hard drive. Over the past few years, though, tape drives have lost some of their popularity to Zip and Jaz drives (go to *http://www.iomega.com* or call 888-516-8467), and other low-cost mass storage devices which are easier to use and more reliable.

Tape drives are, however, still quite common and often used because they can backup entire large hard drives. On the average, tape drives can now backup about 12 GB of data.

93. My Windows backup doesn't recognize my external tape drive. Why not?

A tape drive is only set up for backups, which can only be done with a backup program that is compatible with it. To use the Windows backup, the tape drive needs a designated drive letter. You cannot have a designated drive letter with tape drives so you must use the backup software that was supplied with your tape drive. Check the tape drive manufacturer's web site to see if there is a recent update.

If you're unhappy with this, you may want to check out Dantz Corporation's line of Retrospect tape backup programs. They are easy to use and very reliable. (Go to *http://www.dantz.com* or 1-800-225-4880.)

94. My tape can't hold the full capacity that is advertised. Why not?

When you back up the tape, you can use compression. Compression lets you squeeze more data on the tape. For example, if you have a 4GB hard drive and a 2GB tape drive, you can compress the data from the hard drive at a 2:1 ratio and fit it on the 2GB tape. For more information on tape compression, see question 95.

95. Should I use software compression when doing backups?

This is a judgment call; there are some risks. The advantage is that software compression lets you put more data on a tape. This saves money on tapes and can speed up the backup process because it's actually moving a smaller amount of data. However, it may render your backup incompatible with other tape drives or systems. This means that if you upgrade your computer and replace your tape drive, you may not be able to retrieve data from your tapes, because many software programs use different, often incompatible, compression algorithms. So, if you use compression, you may have more trouble moving your tapes from machine to machine.

96. When I try to restore files from my tape, the backups that appear on my hard drive show today's system date instead of the original file dates that show on the tape drive. Why is it doing this?

This is a function of the operating system that at this time is impossible to change. The only real alternative is to print out the file information on the backup and use the hard copy as a reference. Of course, this only works if your backup software allows you to print this information.

97. I'm getting error messages "No Tape Drive Found." What can be wrong?

- Your software may not be detecting your tape drive.

- Make sure the power and cable connections are properly connected.

- Insert a tape in the drive to see if the light comes on and the tape cartridge starts to spin.

- Make sure the tape manufacturer supports the software you are using.

- If you're using a notebook computer, you should NOT connect a tape drive to a docking station. The tape drive should be connected directly to the parallel port on the back of your notebook.

- You may have a loose data ribbon cable. Check your cable connections.

- You could have an incompatible floppy disk controller (FDC), a lack of support for a third drive, or an improper data cable installation. Check the disk controller manual or the manufacturer's web site to check these.

- The backup software may be malfunctioning. Exit the program or restart the computer to make sure no unwanted processes are running.

- The computer's driver could be in conflict with other backup software.

- You could have external hardware interference. If you're running the drive through an AB switch box, check to see if it's set to the proper port. Also, check your manual to see if this is acceptable. Some tape drives will not function unless the drive is directly connected to the computer.

- Your tape drive may be defective. Contact the manufacturer or the store where you bought the drive.

Definitions:

Docking Station: A type of bay that provides additional external ports for laptops. Laptops generally plug into a docking station for network connection, printers, and other external devices.

Floppy Disk Controller (FDC): A device that manages the flow of data between a computer and peripherals. Specific devices have their own kinds of controllers. PCs come with controllers for standard built-in devices such as hard drives, keyboards, and monitors, but other peripherals may require expansion cards with new controllers.

Parallel Port: Also called printer ports, because of what is usually attached to them (although you can hook tape backup units, CD-ROM drives, scanners, and other devices into parallel ports).

98. I'm getting "Read," "Write," and/or "Compare Errors." What can be wrong?

• Routine maintenance will help extend the life of your tape drive and increase reliability.

• Operate the drive in a clean, dust-free environment.

• Never apply a lubricant to the drive.

• Clean the tape drive head every month or after each eight hours of continuous read/write operations.

The errors can consist of any of the following:

Error Codes	Error Codes	Error Message
03: Bad block	257: Unusable tape	File is larger than expected
04: Blank block	258: Bad tape	(compare)
05: Deleted block	260: Volume directory full	Error correction failed
07: Seek error	261: Media error recovery	(backup or restore)
09: Format failed	unsuccessful	Unable to read tape header
11: Invalid rate	262: Reached end of volume	(catalog rebuild)
13: Invalid tape	264: Error updating tape	
18: Tape despooled	268: Unformatted tape	
19: Write protect	269: Unknown tape format	

Often, the tape itself is the direct cause of read and write errors. You can retension the tape cartridge regularly to eliminate the possibility of this occurring. Retensioning winds the tape forward to the end and back to even out tensions and alignment.

If there are any damaged or corrupted data sectors on your cartridge, you will need to reformat the tape cartridge. You can also try another cartridge to verify if this is a tape-related problem.

You can also try to slow down the tape drive speed by turning burst mode off and selecting the "most compatible operation" option that appears on most backup software.

Some additional reasons why you can get read/write errors are the following:

- Electrical interference: Fluorescent lights, electronic magnets, or other types of electrical devices may be causing problems for your tape drive. Make sure that these types of devices are at least three feet away from the drive.

- Incompatible floppy disk controller (FDC): Your drive may not be compatible with the controller that is used to run the drive. Check with the drive manufacturer for a list of compatible controllers.

- Incompatible media type: Verify that you're using the correct type of tape. Check your tape drive's installation manual for recommended tapes.

- Defective cartridge: Check whether the cartridge is defective by trying another tape.

99. My backup program locks up during backups. Why would it do this?

Your system has become unresponsive; you can't access menu items in Windows and lose keyboard or mouse control. You will need to restart the computer. You may even get the Blue Screen of Death (BSD). This can happen because there is a system/software lockup, which happens with a drive conflict or a program malfunction.

Many programs that run in the background (like screen savers, anti-virus, or non-Microsoft memory managers) are often the problem. It is recommended that you not run any other application while your backup is in progress. The best way to troubleshoot a system lockup problem is temporarily to disable any programs currently loaded in your system memory.

Hard disk problems can also cause system lock up occasionally. Run a hard disk diagnostic utility such as ScanDisk and repair any error it might find. The path to this utility is going to the Start menu, Programs, Accessories, and System tools.

In the unlikely event that the problem persists, perform a clean install of your operating system and reinstall the backup software. If you feel you're not up to this task, let a professional technician handle the problem.

Some additional reasons why software locks up:

- Corrupted program files: Run ScanDisk or Norton Utilities. To run ScanDisk, do the following:

  1. Turn off all other programs.

  2. Start Windows Explorer.

  3. Right-click on the hard drive letter.

  4. Click on Properties.

  5. Click on the Tools tab.

  6. Click on the Check Now button in the Error-checking status area.

  7. Click on the Standard radio button.

  8. Click on the Start button.

  9. After completing this, click on the Thorough radio button.

  10. Click on the Options button.

  11. Click on the System Area Only button.

  12. Click on the OK button.

  13. Click on the Start button.

  14. Click on the Options button.

  15. Click on the Data Area Only button.

  16. Click on the OK button.

17. Click on the Start button.

18. Click on Close.

- Corrupted data block on the tape: Most likely, the tape is bad; replace it with a new one.

- Defective system hardware (e.g., memory chip, hard drive): Use a program like Norton Utilities.

Definitions:

Blue Screen of Death (BSD): A Windows error that locks up your computer and turns the screen blue. In most BSD cases, your only option is to reboot the computer.

ScanDisk: A Windows 95 and Windows 98 utility that detects and repairs errors on the hard drive. The Standard scanning option searches for corrupted files. The Thorough scanning option checks individual sectors.

100. My tape backups seem to be really slow lately. What can be the problem?

The data transfer rate for your tape drive can fluctuate depending on the following:

- Available memory

- CPU speed

- Hardware and software configuration

- Type of data cartridges

- Floppy controller

To achieve top performance:

- Disable any programs running in the background—this can seriously reduce the data transfer rate by tapping your system resources.

These programs include screen savers, anti-virus programs, background fax software, disk caching utilities, and voice mail.

- Your backup software should have an option for reforming the tape. Try it.

- If the tape is old, replace it; it may be worn down. Damaged sectors on the tape often cause the tape drive to re-read the information numerous times. This can sometimes increase backup time by 50 percent or more.

- Cleaning the tape head regularly will allow data transfer at normal throughput. Refer to your tape drive manual on how to care for the drive properly.

- Reinstall the backup software. Corrupted program files can sometimes cause abnormal behavior, such as a slow transfer rate.

- Sometimes the Compression Type selected in the backup software will affect the throughput of your tape drive. See questions 94 and 95 to learn more about data compression.

- If the average file size you're attempting to back up is more than 2 MB, the transfer rate will decrease.

Definitions:

Throughput: The rated speed at which the computer processes information.

101. The parallel port tape drive is not detected under Windows 95 and Windows 98. Why not?

Check to see if the parallel port is set in Extended Capabilities Port (ECP) mode. You can do this by changing the parallel port to either bidirectional or Enhanced Parallel Port (EPP). To determine which mode the parallel port is set for, check the computer's Basic Input/Output System (BIOS) or your computer documentation.

If you're using Windows 95 or Windows 98, refresh the tape drive to ensure that the computer is aware of the drive. To do this:

1. Click on the Start button, Settings, Control Panel, and then the System icon.

2. Click on the Device Manager tab.

3. Double-click on the tape drive.

4. Click the Refresh button. If the computer doesn't show your tape drive, it may not have been set up properly.

To set up the tape drive:

1. Click on the Start button, Settings, Control Panel, and then the Add New Hardware icon.

2. Click on the Next button.

3. From here, follow the on-screen prompts.

NOTE: If you still have problems after installing the driver, check the tape drive manufacturer's web site for updated files or resources.

If the problem is still not resolved, refer to the unit's hardware troubleshooting section for additional information.

Definitions:

Extended Capabilities Port (ECP): Provides enhanced two-way communication between computer and peripheral. Microsoft and Hewlett-Packard developed the ECP specification to extend the speed of the parallel port and to provide two-way throughput. Like the supercharged EPP spec, ECP is fast. Windows 95 directly supports ECP.

Enhanced Parallel Port (EPP): Allows computers to communicate to hard disks, tape backup units, CD-ROM drives, and other mass-storage devices that use parallel ports Developed by Intel, Xircom, Zenith, and many other companies, the EPP spec builds on the design of the parallel port by adding two-way communications and faster exchange of peripheral-to-computer communication.

102. The tape in the tape drive has despooled (unraveled). What can be wrong?

Despooling can be caused by one of two situations.

1. The tape cartridge is incorrect for the tape drive. Make sure you have the right one.

2. The tape cartridge may need to be retensioned or the tape drive is not detecting the End of Tape (EOT) marker.

To determine which of these two is the problem, open the lid on the front of the tape and look for the actual tape. If the tape is not present, then the tape drive is causing the despooling and needs to be replaced. If the tape is present, then the tape cartridge needs to be retensioned.

• To troubleshoot your tape drive:

1. Reset the tape drive by disconnecting and then reconnecting it to the power source and try to simulate the error.

2. Make sure the tape drive is connected directly to the parallel port. The tape drive will not work properly if connected through a switch box, dongle, or software key.

3. Check all power connections to the tape drive by inserting a tape into the tape drive. On most tape drives, when a tape is inserted, the light on the drive will flash and the tape should start spinning. If the tape drive does not respond and the power connections are connected, get in touch with the drive's manufacturer for technical support or warranty replacement.

4. Disconnect or turn off any bidirectional printer that may be connected to the computer.

5. Check all cable connections from the tape drive to the drive interface (either the floppy disk controller or the card). Make sure connections are secure and all pins are connected properly. Damaged pins may cause the cables to function improperly; they may need to be replaced.

Definitions:

Bidirectional printer: A printer that can print both left to right and right to left.

Dongle: A copy protection device that comes with a software package. A dongle includes a hardware interface key without which the software will not function. The key also can impede software duplication.

Additional definitions:

Institute of Electrical and Electronics Engineers (IEEE): Not-for-profit U.S. engineering organization that develops, defines, and reviews standards within the electronics and computer science industries.

Zip Drives

There are so many Zip drives around that they may eventually replace the floppy disk. Because of this, we have decided to dedicate a single section specifically to Zip drive problems.

103. My computer doesn't recognize my USB Zip drive. Why not?

• Your software may be older and therefore incompatible.

• Go to Iomega's Web site and download a copy of the latest version, *http://www.iomega.com.*

Definitions:

Universal Serial Bus (USB): An interface for peripherals. This low-speed hardware device supports digital video and can be disconnected without turning the computer off.

104. Why is my Zip drive making repetitive clicking sounds?

It's normal for a zip drive to click when a zip disk is inserted, ejected, or accessed from it, but repetitive clicking is a symptom of a damaged drive or disk.

Contact Iomega tech support at 1-888-4IOMEGA (1-888-446-6342) to confirm the problem.

105. I carry my Zip drive and disks around all the time. What can I do to prevent them from getting damaged?

Eject disks before transporting your Zip drive. This will let the drive heads park, which puts them in a neutral position. The drive heads are what read and write to the disks. Parking the heads makes sure that they don't move during transport and damage the disk or the drive.

Some maintenance actions you can take to sustain the quality of your drive are the following:

1. Don't drop the drive because it may damage both the interior and exterior structure.

2. Make sure to transport and store disks only in disk cases.

3. Run the Iomega Tools diagnostics program tests to check the integrity of the Zip heads and Zip media. Be sure to use a blank formatted disk while running these tests.

4. Iomega doesn't charge for technical support when a Zip drive or disk is found to be defective and under warranty; however, it does charge for out-of-warranty technical support calls on the drives themselves.

106. Can I use Zip 250 MB disks in a Zip 100MB drive?

No. The 100MB Zip drives were not designed for the 250MB disks. If you try it, the drive will automatically eject the disk. However, you can use the 100MB disks in the 250MB Zip drive.

107. Can I reassign my Zip drive to drive letter B (drive B:)?

No. This assignment will cause the computer not to recognize the Zip drive.

NOTE: Iomega does not support using the Zip drive when controlled by the computer's Basic Input/Output System (BIOS). Iomega only supports Zip drives being controlled by the Iomega driver. Therefore, the Zip drive must be assigned to a drive letter D: through Z:

108. I'm trying to access my Zip drive but I keep getting an error message ("Cannot find Tools disk") in Windows 95 and Windows 98. What's wrong?

This occurs when the Iomega Tools software fails to assign a drive letter to your Zip drive. The problem may be that the version of Iomega Tools is an older version. You will need to download a newer version for Windows 98/95 at Iomega's Web site: *http:\\www.iomega.com*. To download the newer version:

1. Go the Iomega web site.

2. Click on Software Download (to the left).

3. Click on IomegaWare 2.2.1 (to the right). As of April 2000, Version 2.2.1 is the newest Tools Package version.

4. Download the IomegaWare Windows or Macintosh version (the Windows version appears above the Macintosh version).

5. Fill out the demographic information.

6. Click on the Submit button.

7. Follow the instructions from there.

8. Once you've installed the new version of Core IomegaWare Tools Package, you should no longer receive the error message.

NOTE: If you still have difficulties call Iomega for tech support help at 1-888-4IOMEGA (1-888-446-6342).

109. How do I compress the files I copy to my Zip drive?

- Files can be compressed with a compression utility such as WinZip or PKZip.

- Files must first be compressed and then copied or moved to the Zip disk.

- Iomega does not support any type of drive compression software being used on the actual Zip disk.

- If the actual Zip disk is compressed, the integrity of the data and the disk may be may be compromised. This can result in your files being unrecoverable.

Definitions:

PKZip (also called PKUnzip): A utility from PKWARE for unzipping and zipping files. Go to *http://www.pkware.com*. (PK is an acronym for Phillip Katz.)

WinZip: A utility from Nico Mac Computing for unzipping and zipping files. Go to *http://www.winzip.com*.

110. I should have plenty of space on my Zip disk. So why am I getting an error message ("Disk is full")?

You may have exceeded the file limit set by your operating system. Or you may have a defective disk. It may also be possible that you have files in the Recycle Bin that have not been deleted. See number 74.

111. How do I correct the error message in question 110?

Check that the disk has enough room available to accommodate the files you want to copy. Remember that the number of files when you first open your Iomega drive cannot exceed the limit set by your operating system. If the number of files you want to copy exceeds this limit, you will have to move individual files into another folder on your hard drive. This will temporarily reduce the number of files you have showing.

Make a new folder on your Iomega disk. You may then move the files back to your Iomega disk. To do this:

1. Open Windows Explorer.

2. Click on the hard drive letter.

3. Click on the File drop-down menu.

4. Click on New and then on Folder.

5. Type a name for the new folder.

6. Press your Enter button.

7. Click and drag two or more files from the root directory of your Iomega drive into the new folder. (By click and drag, we mean move the file/folder, not copy it.)

8. Click and drag the new folder from your hard drive to your Iomega drive.

9. Click and drag other files relating to your Iomega drive to this new folder.

112. I did the procedure in question 111, but I'm still having problems. What do I do now?

Try shutting the computer, the Iomega drive, and all peripherals completely off and then restart them. If this doesn't succeed, try several different disks. If the error message occurs on only one disk, reformat that disk (but remember that formatting will remove all data from the disk).

If you get the error message with more than one disk or the disk will not format, contact Iomega at 1-888-4-IOMEGA (1-888-446-6342). If you are outside the United States, you can go to the Web site at *http://www.iomega.com* and search for a worldwide location and/or phone number.

113. I am convinced something is wrong with my Zip drive. How can I test it?

Iomega offers a software utility that tests the internal workings of the Zip heads and Zip media. Take a blank, formatted disk and do the following:

1. If you're a Windows 95, Windows 98, or Windows 2000 user, click on the Windows Explorer icon.

2. Right-mouse-click on the Zip drive icon.

3. Click on Properties.

4. Click on the Diagnostics tab.

5. Click on the Diagnose Now button to start the Diagnostic function test.

When you click on the Diagnose Now button, the software will start a drive function test and provide a report of either Passed or Failed. If the test fails, contact Iomega technical support at 1-888-4-IOMEGA (1-888-446-6342) or at *http://www.iomega.com*. If it says but you still get repetitive clicking, contact Iomega Technical Support.

1. Macintosh users, open the Iomega Tools folder.

2. Double-click on the Tools icon.

3. Click on the icon showing the two drives.

4. Click on the Push to Diagnose button.

When you click on the Push to Diagnose button in Mac OS, the software will start a drive function test and provide a report of either Passed or Failed. If the test fails, contact Iomega technical support at 1-888-4-IOMEGA (1-888-446-6342) or at *http://www.iomega.com*. If the report says Passed and you still get repetitive clicking, contact Iomega Technical Support.

Chapter 2
The Internet

SEARCH ENGINES

1. First, before we discuss search engines, what's the difference between the Internet and the World Wide Web?

The Internet is a global network. To use an analogy, you could view the Internet as the phone lines, cables, telephone poles, etc., that help you make a call. The World Wide Web (WWW/ Web) is one of the services of the Internet. When people say they are in the Web, it makes as much sense as saying I'm "in" the phone. Other services in the Internet include e-mail, file transfer, and newsgroups.

2. What are search engines?

In a nutshell, search engines are servers that run software, also called software robots (bots) or spiders. These engines search the Web for sites/pages that match your query. To use an analogy, if you go into a library, you have to have some way of finding the book you want. You'll either use a card catalog system, a computer program, or the reference librarian. Just as the books are organized in a certain way (the Dewey decimal system), sites on the Web are organized in a certain way, with key words (meta tags) to help you find them.

Some call search engines portals, which is not entirely accurate; portals are information sites or entry points in the Web to lead you to the information you desire. For instance, Disney.com is a portal. For more information on search engines, try *http://www.searchenginewatch.com* as a start.

3. Is a search engine the same as an Internet Service Provider (ISP)?

No. An ISP is the company (usually using the phone lines) that connects you and your computer to the Internet (the outside electronic world). The ISP is the mail carrier or delivery person who acts as the interface between you and your friends. The search engine is like a phone book to help you find an address or phone number.

4. Is Netscape Navigator (Navigator) or Internet Explorer (IE) a search engine?

No. Navigator and IE are interfaces inside your computer that allow you and your computer to communicate with the Internet (the outside electronic world). Here's another analogy: Navigator or IE is your interpreter to the Web (since you don't speak computer). The ISP is a delivery system in the Internet, just like Airborne Express or the Postal Service in the real world. Now, Navigator and IE have their own versions of search engines inside your computer.

5. Okay. Now what's this "HTTP" I keep seeing?

HTTP stands for HyperText Transfer Protocol. It's a set of standards, or protocols, used so that information can be accurately exchanged on the Web. For example, the Postal Service wants us all to address our letters in a certain way to ensure that they get there; computers use HTTP to make sure web pages and sites are transmitted correctly (see information below about HTML).

HTTP is especially useful in creating hyperlinks (links or connections to other web sites and/or pages), but other protocols exist. File Transfer Protocol (FTP) is used to help computers accurately send and receive files, for instance. You will also find Post Office Protocol (POP), Simple Mail Transport Protocol (SMTP), transmission control protocol/internet protocol (TCP/IP)—to many to discuss here.

6. Is HTTP the same as HyperText Markup Language (HTML), another acronym I often see?

No. HTML is a programming language used to construct a web site. One of the uses of HTML is to mark the site and all the hyperlinks within it. If you want to see what the code is for a particular site in Netscape Navigator:

1. Click on the View drop-down menu.

2. Click on Page View, or click on Page Source.

Web sites are text pages with lots of graphics and hyperlinks added. HTML uses special codes (tags) that format the page to be more interactive and useful than just plain text.

7. Okay. So, is HTML the only programming language used to create web sites?

No. Others exist, such as Standard Generalized Markup Language (SGML) and eXtensible Markup Language (XML). But you don't need to know a language to create a Web page; you can use software like Adobe PageMill, Microsoft FrontPage, or Claris Home Page.

8. What are the popular search engines?

There are too many to discuss here. We discuss five of the most popular in questions 13 to 17. Others include Ask Jeeves, Dogpile, HotBot, InfoSeek, LookSmart, Mamma, Snap, and Webcrawler. More are being added all the time. Each claims to search more sites than the other engines.

Each engine has a different way of searching and indexing the Web for sites matching your search requirements. Users may prefer Ask Jeeves because you can query this engine with a question written in English; you don't have to know anything about Boolean operators and the rest.

9. What are metasearch engines?

Since there are so many search engines, people have created search engines to search other search engines. More bang for your buck, so to speak. To use an analogy, a metasearch engine is your researcher, who has hired a group of researchers. Instead of having to talk to all these researchers, you only have to talk to their boss. One popular metasearch engine is MetaCrawler.

10. You keep talking about hyperlinks. What are hyperlinks?

Inside a Web site or a page, you often see a graphic, picture, or underlined word you can double-click on. Once you double-click on it, you'll be taken to another Web site or page. This graphic, picture, or word is a hyperlink. For instance, in the CNN Web site, you could double-click on the underlined word Weather and be taken to the part of the site supplying information on United States weather.

11. How do you search?

The two major methods of searching are by Keyword and by Concept.

* In *keyword searching*, the engine extracts words it believes to be significant and useful. This style of searching will only find sites with the words you specified in your search. An example is Infoseek.

* In *concept-based searching*, the engine tries to determine what you mean. This system is more complex, employing artificial intelligence algorithms and linguistic approaches too complicated to discuss here. The concept approach may find sites that don't have the words you specified even though the meaning is identical. An example is Excite.

Part of the problem with both of these is the overwhelming quantity of information on the Web. Some search engines index every word in each document, which is ultimately useless. Some discriminate by upper and lower case. Some searches include the stop words (e.g., a, an, the, and). Others only search the titles, headings, and subheadings of a document. A lot depends, too, on how the Web designer has tagged the site.

To circumvent these problems, use a refined search. For instance, in MetaCrawler, you can specify to search by: 1. Any (word); 2. All (words); or 3. Phrase. So, if you wanted information on Georgia's lottery, typed in "Georgia lottery" (without the quotation marks), and requested All, you would receive documents for Georgia, Lottery, and Georgia's lottery. The

Phrase request would save time and reduce the number of irrelevant documents you get.

In other search engines, you can use a variety of advanced search techniques. In Yahoo!, you can refine your search with an exact phrase match, Boolean operators (e.g., AND, OR), and more. AltaVista allows you to search in different languages.

Search engines also use relevancy rankings. In MetaCrawler, each site is ranked by how closely the engine thinks it matches your search criteria, with 1,000 being the most relevant.

12. What are Uniform Resource Locators (URLs)?

URLs are the addresses of (which are also the routes to) web sites. Sometimes you may see a string of four numbers separated by periods. This is the Internet Protocol (IP) address, which is similar to a URL; you don't have to deal with it because URLs, such as *www.cnn.com*, get you right to the site instead of just to the server. The first part of the address (http://) is the protocol and traditionally connects you to a server (e.g., WWW, Gopher, FTP). After that, all you usually need is the domain name (with any necessary subdomains separated by slashes).

13. How do you search on AltaVista?

AltaVista, created in 1995 and now owned by Compaq, allows you to search by:

- Boolean query (in Advanced Search)

- Sort by (in Advanced Search)

- Language (in Advanced Search or the drop-down menu)

- From/To (in Advanced Search) in terms of the publication date

Print out the cheat sheet AltaVista provides. This sheet gives you information on the Boolean operators (AND, OR, AND NOT, and NEAR) and other ways to search the Web.

AltaVista lets you search in 24 languages; it claims access to hundreds of millions of Web pages.

AltaVista also includes a Family Filter to filter out "objectionable material." You can specify where the material is coming from: Multimedia Only, All, or None. You must enter a password to change the settings.

Address: *http://www.altavista.com*

14. How do you search on Excite?

To do refined searches in Excite, you must click on the word More to the right of the search box or Advanced Search at the bottom of the Excite page. Clicking once on the Excite logo takes you to your personalized Excite page. Excite allows you to search by:

- Language (11 choices)

- Advanced Web Search

- Advanced News Search

- Advance Audio/Video Search

- Type of Site

Advanced Web Search lets you add constraints in many combinations: SHOULD contain, MUST contain, and MUST NOT contain. One of these is then combined with: the word(s) and the phrase for the topic you're interested in.

You can also search by Language and Type of Site (domain). The language section allows you to search by country (flag icons), and the type of domain section comprises the .com, .edu, .net, .org, .gov, and .mil domains.

A filter allows you to "Exclude Adult Content."

Finally, you can decide how you want to Display Results. Under the Document heading, you can produce results by Description (Titles only or Titles and summaries) and by Results per page (10, 20, 30, 40, or 50). The Web sites button shows 40 results per page and can't be altered.

Address: *http://www.excite.com*

15. How do you search on Lycos?

Lycos began in June 1995 with a spidering technology that had its beginnings at Carnegie Mellon University. In April 1999, Lycos became the most visited hub. It has an Advanced Search mechanism along with a Multimedia search and Parental Controls.

- *Advanced Search* uses the following: all words (AND match); any words (OR match); and, exact phrase (quoted query).

- *Multimedia Search* checks as follows: All, Pictures, Movies, Streams, and, Sounds.

- *Parental Controls* employs software packages like SearchGuard to protect your children from information and visuals you don't want them to have.

You can also search the Web by Content, Page Field, Language, and Link Reforms:

- *Content* allows you to choose specific types of documents on the Web, such as books, downloads, or music.

- *Page Field* searches for documents by fields such as by Title, URL, or Host/domain.

- *Language* allows you to choose one of 24 languages.

- *Link Referrals* lets you search for documents that link to your site, such as by Your URL, Search Only this Host, and Exclude this Host. Address: *http://www.lycos.com*

16. How do you search on MetaCrawler?

Erik Selberg and Oren Etzioni released MetaCrawler in June 1995 at the University of Washington. Go2Net took over MetaCrawler's operation about two years later. MetaCrawler uses one server for the text and another for the images of a web page, which increases its speed.

MetaCrawler is a search engine that searches other search engines. Under the search box, you can select one of three buttons: Any, All, and, Phrase.

The Phrase selection will find pages that are the same or nearly identical. MetaCrawler ranks the matches with a numbering system with 1,000 being the most relevant and 0 being the least relevant. Thankfully, MetaCrawler will combine identical pages if they are found by more than one search engine. You can also use Power Search, which gives you five options:

- Select which engines to search (12 are available)

- Select domain/origin (Everywhere, U.S. educational sites, Asia, etc.)

- Speed/Timeout (maximum time to wait for results: from Fastest to two minutes)

- Quantity (results per page and results per source: 10, 20, or 30)

- View Results (by) relevance, site, source

You have many options to customize your search to remember your settings for next time. In addition to those just above, there is:

- Default Interface (format of start page: normal search, power search, low bandwidth)

- Keyword Default (any, all, phrase)

- Auto-focus (automatically places cursor in the search box: on or off)

- Sticky (saves search parameters: on or off)

- Search by Country (25 choices)
      Address: *http://www.metacrawler/index.html*

17. How do I search on Yahoo!?

David Filo and Jerry Yang began Yahoo! in April 1994. (Yahoo! is an acronym for Yet Another Hierarchical Officious Oracle.) The Yahoo! files have now moved in with Netscape, to the betterment of both parties.

Yahoo! has an Advanced Search. You select one of four search methods by clicking on the Advanced Search button to the right of the search box:

- Intelligent default

- An exact phrase match

- Matches on all words (AND)

- Matches on any word (OR).

You can select one of two search areas: Yahoo! categories or Web sites.

You can specify time how recent articles should be, with ranges from one day to four years.

Finally, you can specify how many matches per page you want: 10, 20, 50, or 100.

If you click on Advanced Search Syntax at the bottom of the Advanced Search page, Yahoo! will guide you in refining your search. If you're not sure how to use Yahoo, click on How to use Yahoo! Search. Yahoo! lets you use quotation marks and plus or minus signs to refine the search. Unlike some of the other search engines, Yahoo! lets you use an asterisk (*) as a wild card: if you typed app*, you might get articles on application, apprentice, and so on.

Yahoo! uses three methods to rank its results: Multiple Keyword Matches, Document Section Weighting, and Generality of Category.
Address: *http://www.yahoo.com*

Definitions:

AND: AND is a Boolean operator that combines words into a phrase when searching for information. For instance, if you enter Austin AND Powers, the search engine will look for the phrase Austin Powers or documents with both words in them.

AND NOT: AND NOT is a Boolean operator identical to NOT. Some search engines employ NOT; others use AND NOT.

Boolean operators: The combination of words that must be used for searching various databases, the Web, etc. You must always capitalize them. For more information on Boolean operators, try *http://www.imagescape.com/helpweb/www/seek.html* as a start.

Minus sign: The minus sign is identical to the NOT Boolean operator.

NEAR: A Boolean operator designed to find documents with similar phrasing.

NOT: A Boolean operator that excludes a term in your search and reduces the number of documents the search engine will find for you. For instance, if you type Beetles NOT Volkswagen, you'll get articles about the insect but not about the car.

OR: A Boolean operator that gives the search engine the choice of finding at least one of the words. For instance, if you type Apple OR Computer, you'll get information on apples, the Apple Computer Company, and computers.

Plus sign: Identical to the AND Boolean operator.

Quotation marks: Some search engines use quotation marks to specify an exact phrase. For instance, if you type Apple Computer alone, you'll get articles about apples, Apple Computer, and computers. If you type "Apple Computer" (using the quotation marks), you should only get articles about the company.

Server: A computer with a large power supply and cabinet capacity. A server is also a computer that makes printer or communication services available to other computers (network stations).

NETSCAPE COMMUNICATOR

The major features of Netscape Communicator (version 4.7) are (there are many minor features):

- Netscape Composer: Helps you design your own web pages.

- Netscape Messenger: Helps you send and receive electronic mail (e-mail).

• Netscape Navigator: Helps you surf the World Wide Web.

• Netscape Newsgroups: Helps you enter newsgroups and share information with their users.

If you need technical support after you download the software, remember that none of it is free. Keep copious notes of what you type in and/or select as you load or download Netscape. Remember the preferences, etc., in case you need to change certain characteristics.

18. Which is better: Netscape Communicator or Internet Explorer (IE)?

It depends whom you ask. One of us prefer Netscape because he finds it easier to use, it attaches files with fewer glitches, and it interfaces with the Web better. Netscape also deletes previously visited web sites and accumulated history files more easily and its housecleaning abilities are continually enhanced. Of course, each version of both takes a leapfrog over its competitor.

19. I want to install Netscape Communicator. How do I do it?

You have two choices: you can download it or you can order the CD-ROM. Your computer must have at least 35 MB of hard disk space and at least 16 MB of Random Access Memory (RAM).

To download Netscape from the Internet:

1. Pick a time when you have at least an hour free (depending on the speed of your computer, modem, telephone lines, etc.).

2. Go to the Netscape Web site, which is *http://home.netscape.com.*

3. Click on the Download graphic.

4. Follow the instructions from there.

To order Netscape on CD-ROM, go to its Web site or call (toll-free) 800-638-7483 or (not toll-free) 650-937-3777. To load Netscape from a CD-ROM:

1. Make sure you've closed all other applications.

2. Put the CD-ROM in its drive. Follow the instructions from there.

If nothing happens after you put the CD-ROM in the drive:

1. Click on Start and then Run.

2. Type D:/ (or, whatever letter you use for your CD-ROM drive).

3. Click on the Browse button.

4. Look for a Setup file.

5. Double-click on this file (which will be entered into the text line in the Run dialog box.

6. Click on OK, and follow instructions.

Netscape Communicator Customization

20. Netscape doesn't seem to work the way I want it. How do I adjust it?

You have many options for this, but the quickest is through Preferences. We've broken your question down by preference, producing the detailed questions that we answer next. Many of these changes can be executed in the Preferences dialog box (found in the Edit drop-down menu), which is why we start there. But first:

• To change software (Composer, Navigator, etc.) you want to appear when you open Netscape:

1. Open Netscape (you don't have to be connected to the Internet).

2. Click on the Edit drop-down menu, and then Preferences. (Or press Alt+E, E.)

3. Double-click on Appearance.

4. To the right, click on the Navigator, Messenger, Composer, or Calendar checkbox. (We suggest you choose only one; you can navigate to the others easily as needed without keeping them open.)

5. Click on OK.

- To change the look of the toolbars:

    1. Open Netscape (you don't have to be connected to the Internet).

    2. Click on the Edit drop-down menu, and then Preferences. (Or press Alt+E, E.)

    3. Double-click on Appearance.

    4. To the right and below, click on either Pictures and Text, Pictures Only, or Text Only buttons.

    5. Click on OK.

21. I want to change the appearance of the fonts. How do I do it?

- To change the look of the font in messages, etc:

    1. Open Netscape (you don't have to be connected to the Internet).

    2. Click on the Edit drop-down menu, and then Preferences. (Or press Alt+E, E.)

    3. Double-click on Appearance.

    4. Click on Fonts (underneath Appearance).

    5. Click on the drop-down arrows to the right of Variable Width Font and also of Fixed Width Font to adjust font type and font size.

    6. Click on OK.

- If you're getting e-mail with odd font types, to change the font to match the type you use:

  1. Open Netscape (you don't have to be connected to the Internet).

  2. Click on the Edit drop-down menu, and then Preferences. (Or press Alt+E, E.)

  3. Double-click on Appearance.

  4. Click on Fonts (underneath Appearance).

  5. Click on the first buttons to the right and below that state the following: Use my default fonts, overriding document-specific fonts.

  6. Click on OK.

- While we don't suggest changing the font colors from their default settings, you can do it this way:

  1. Open Netscape (you don't have to be connected to the Internet).

  2. Click on the Edit drop-down menu, and then Preferences. (Or press Alt+E, E.)

  3. Double-click on Appearance.

  4. Click on Colors (underneath Appearance).

  5. Double-click on one of the four color boxes. This will activate the color dialog box, from which you can select a new color or customize and create your own color.

  6. Click on OK.

- If you're getting e-mail with odd font colors and want to change this:

  1. Open Netscape (you don't have to be connected to the Internet).

2. Click on the Edit drop-down menu, and then Preferences. (Or press Alt+E, E.)

3. Double-click on Appearance.

4. Click on Colors (underneath Appearance).

5. Click on the checkbox to the right and below that state: Always use my colors, overriding document.

6. Click on OK.

Netscape Navigator Customization

While you can alter the language specification and turn on or off the Smart Browsing capability (leave it on), most of what you want to customize is in Preferences' Navigator dialog box.

22. I want to change or select a home page in Navigator. How do I do this?

Perhaps you want to select a home page with few graphics because the more graphics a page has, the longer it will take to load; for instance, *www.cnn.com* will take longer to load than, say, *www.metacrawler.com*. To select a particular home page:

1. Open Netscape (you don't have to be connected to the Internet).

2. Click on the Edit drop-down menu, and then Preferences. (Or press Alt+E, E.)

3. Click on Navigator once (double-clicking on Navigator will bring you choices for Smart Browsing, etc., which does not need to be discussed here).

4. In the location text box, type the address you want, for instance, *http://www.metacrawler.com.*

5. Click on OK.

If you're on the Internet and at the site of choice, do the following:

1. Have Netscape open and have the web site selected that you want to be the home page.

2. Click on the Edit drop-down menu, and then Preferences. (Or, press Alt+E, E.)

3. Click on Navigator once (double-clicking on Navigator will bring you choices for Smart Browsing, etc., which doesn't need to be discussed here).

4. To the right and under the Home Page section, click on the Use Current Page button. This will select the current web site as your home page. Try not to select a web site with many graphics and icons because the more there are, the more time you wait for the page to load.

5. Click on OK.

Definitions:

Uniform Resource Locator (URL): The address for a web site on the Internet. Most URLs begin with the code http:\\, which stands for HyperText Transfer Protocol.

23. I want to keep my folders/files cleaned. How do I do this?

Good idea! Unlike previous editions of Netscape Communicator and many editions of Internet Explorer, the newest versions of Netscape let you keep its files clean without you having to do all the housecleaning.

To keep the files cleaned:

1. Open Netscape (you don't have to be connected to the Internet).

2. Click on the Edit drop-down menu, and then Preferences. (Or, press Alt+E, E.)

3. Click on Navigator once (double-clicking on Navigator will bring you choices for Smart Browsing, etc., which doesn't need to be discussed here).

4. Go to the History section to the right and below. Type 0 (zero) if you want the web pages cleaned as soon as you close Netscape.

5. To do your own housecleaning, click on the Clear History button.

6. To do more housecleaning, click on the Clear Location Bar button.

7. Click on OK.

CAUTION: These files aren't automatically deleted unless you instruct the software to do so. You can't clear them even if you go to Windows Explorer. You must do the housekeeping from the Preferences dialog box.

24. Can I keep the files cleaned elsewhere?

Yes. To avoid unnecessary usage of memory:

1. Open Netscape (you don't have to be connected to the Internet).

2. Click on the Edit drop-down menu, and then Preferences. (Or, press Alt+E, E.)

3. Double-click on Advanced.

4. Click on Cache.

5. Click on the Clear Memory Cache button and click on OK.

6. Click on the Clear Disk Cache button and click on OK.

7. In the Memory Cache and Disk Cache boxes, increase the number in the textbox. I had enough memory to type in 65536 (a multiple of two). The more memory you add here, the faster you may be able to surf the Internet.

NOTE: Remember to clear the caches after you've completed surfing the Internet. In this way, you'll have the computer as clean as possible when you enter the Web next time. You can also keep files cleaned by deleting them from the Trash bin along with the Inbox and Sent bins. A quick way to get rid of files in the Trash bin is the keyboard command Alt+F, Y.

Netscape Mail and Newsgroups Customization

Many of the subcategories here are technical; you don't want to change, for instance, your identity or mail servers unless you know what you're doing. Usually, you should contact your Internet Service Provider (ISP) to see if you can make these changes and to learn how to do that.

Definitions:

Internet Service Provider (ISP): A company that connects you and your computer to the Internet (the outside electronic world).

25. I want to know when I have e-mail. What can I do?

To set the computer to alert you about incoming mail, do the following:

1. Open Netscape (you don't have to be connected to the Internet).

2. Click on the Edit drop-down menu, and then Preferences. (Or, press Alt+E, E.)

3. Click on Mail & Newsgroups.

4. Below and to the right, click on the Play sound when messages arrive checkbox.

5. Click on OK.

26. I want to add my company name, address, and phone number to every my e-mail I send. How do I do this?

To add your signature text:

1. Open Netscape (you don't have to be connected to the Internet).

2. Click on the Edit drop-down menu, and then Preferences. (Or, press Alt+E, E.)

3. Double-click on Mail & Newsgroups.

4. Click on Identity (below Mail & Newsgroups).

5. Type in where Netscape should find the signature file in the Signature File textbox. (For instance, I created my signature file and put it in a folder I called Work Docs.)

6. Click on OK.

27. Wait a minute. How do I create my own signature file?

I used WordPad because it's the easiest to use. To create your own signature file using WordPad:

1. Click on the Start button, Program, Accessories, and then WordPad.

2. Type in your name, address, and whatever information you want to include. Don't worry about special frills, fonts, etc.

3. Save this file where you can remember its location (and back it up), so Netscape can find it.

28. How do I change the layout of Netscape Messenger?

Do the following:

1. Open Netscape (you don't have to be connected to the Internet).

2. Click on the Edit drop-down menu, and then Preferences. (Or press Alt+E, E.)

3. Double-click on Mail & Newsgroups.

4. Click on Window Settings (below Mail & Newsgroups).

5. Click on one of the two buttons to the right.

6. Click on OK.

NOTE: You can also put your pointer on the borders between the three window panes in Netscape Messenger and click and drag them to select your own dimensions for receiving and sending e-mail messages.

29. How do I get a receipt when I send an e-mail message?

To get a receipt:

1. Open Netscape (you don't have to be connected to the Internet).

2. Click on the Edit drop-down menu, and then Preferences. (Or, press Alt+E, E.)

3. Double-click on Mail & Newsgroups.

4. Click on Return Receipts (below Mail & Newsgroups).

5. Click on the Both types of receipt radio button.

6. Click on OK.

CAUTION: If the receiver has a different setting for receipts, you may still not get one even if you set the return receipt selections.

30. I don't want Internet advertisers to have information about me. How do I prevent it?

To stop information about yourself from reaching their sites, you can turn off the cookies. To do this, do the following:

1. Open Netscape (you don't have to be connected to the Internet).

2. Click on the Edit drop-down menu, and then Preferences. (Or, press Alt+E, E.)

3. Click on Advanced.

4. Click on Disable cookies button.

5. Click on Warn me before accepting a cookie.

6. Click on OK.

NOTE: Even though you disable the cookies, you should also ask to be warned of cookies because advertisers can detect your surfing movement by simply adding a special single pixel (transparent GIF). And even this stopgap may or may not fully protect you. For more information consult see Consumer Reports (May 2000), pp. 43-50.

CAUTION: Even if you do this, the Internet has an insidious way of sneaking into your computer. Many software manufacturers will let you to check your system to see how much protection your privacy has against the outside world.

31. Help! I'm getting junk e-mail. How do I get rid of it?

First, all junk e-mail companies say you can get off their e-mail mailing list by responding to the address they give you. *Don't respond to them.* This is their way of verifying you exist. *Don't respond.*

Netscape lets you set up filters to stop them from getting to you. To set up the filters:

1. Open Netscape (you don't have to be connected to the Internet).

2. Click on the Edit drop-down menu, and then Message Filters. (Or press Alt+E, I.)

3. Click on the New button.

4. Enter a name into the Filter name textbox, something like Junk Mail 1, Junk Mail 2, etc.

5. In the first textbox below, click on the drop-down arrow and select Sender.

6. In the next textbox to the right, select "is".

7. In the next textbox to the right, enter the e-mail address of the junk e-mail company. If you need to enter more than one junk e-mail address, click on the More button. You can enter up to five addresses. If you need to add more, simply create a new filter (starting from step three).

8. Click on the textbox under the More/Fewer buttons, and select Delete.

9. Click on OK.

NOTE: In this Message Filters dialog box, you can set up many other possibilities for filtration. Investigate this dialog box more extensively as time permits.

32. I'm tired of surfing through all these web sites I don't need. How do I quickly find sites I want?

Netscape helps you find what you're looking for by simply typing the term(s) in its location toolbar. To do this:

1. Connect with your Internet Service Provider (ISP).

2. Open Netscape Navigator.

3. Type in the name/term you want in the location toolbar, which is the textbox to the right of the word Location. For instance, if you want the web site for IBM, type in IBM.

33. I want to organize my bookmarks. How do I do this?

Organizing your bookmarks makes life much easier. You create your own folders and then put sites into the folders. To organize your material:

1. Open Navigator (you don't have to be connected to the Internet). You'll get a message stating that: Netscape is unable to locate the server. Don't worry about it; this is Netscape telling you're not connected.

2. Click on View on the first toolbar.

3. Click on Bookmarks.

4. Click on Edit Bookmarks.

5. Click on a folder.

6. Click and drag the folder to a new location if you want your folders in, say, alphabetical order. Netscape doesn't do this automatically.

7. Or double-click on a folder.

8. Click and drag a web site to a folder by placing it on top of the folder. It will not be automatically alphabetized within the folder.

9. Double-click on the receiving folder so you can click and drag the sites in it until they're organized the way you want them.

NOTE: In this screen, you'll see many folders with plus (+) signs to the left of them (meaning they have subfolders inside). At the top, you should see the main folder, which states: Bookmarks for (your name).

34. How do I delete bookmarks I've never used or no longer use?

To delete web sites:

1. Open Navigator (you don't have to be connected to the Internet for this).

2. Click on View on the first toolbar.

3. Click on Bookmarks.

4. Click on Edit Bookmarks.

5. Double-click on a folder.

6. Click on the web site you want to delete.

7. Press the Delete button on your keyboard. (To delete this site from your computer totally, you'll have to go to the Recycle Bin and delete it from there.)

35. I want to bookmark a site I'm looking at. How do I do this?

To bookmark a site:

1. Connect with your Internet Service Provider (ISP).

2. Open Netscape Navigator.

3. Surf to the site you want to bookmark.

4. Click on the Bookmarks button (underneath View on the top toolbar).

5. Click on Add Bookmark.

NOTE: Once you've clicked on Add Bookmark, the site will not automatically drop into a folder. Follow the instructions in question 33 for clicking and dragging a site to the folder of your choice.

36. How do I create a folder for some sites I've found?

To create your own folder:

1. Open Navigator (you don't have to be connected to the Internet for this).

2. Click on View on the first toolbar.

3. Click on Bookmarks.

4. Click on Edit Bookmarks.

5. Click on the top line, which states: Bookmarks for (your name).

6. Click on File from the drop-down menu.

7. Click on New Folder.
8. Type in the name you want to give the folder.

9. Click on OK.

INTERNET EXPLORER 5.X

Internet Explorer (IE) is Microsoft's default web browser, but if you don't have it we'll show you how to find and install it from the Internet or from a Microsoft CD. Then we address common questions about specific tasks and using e-mail through Microsoft Outlook Express. If you don't like Internet Explorer, we provide instructions on disabling some of its more annoying features or removing it from your system.

37. I want Internet Explorer. How do I get it?

You need a Pentium processor or better, Windows 95 or later, and at least 45 MB of free disk space for the installation process (once installed, it takes a little less space). You'll need the installation file.

To get it via the Internet:

1. Allow plenty of time (depending on the power and speed of your computer) since this could take a few hours or more.

2. Go to *www.microsoft.com*.

3. Click on Downloads from the blue title bar.

4. Click on the drop-down arrow to the right of Product Name.

5. Select the latest version of Internet Explorer.

6. Click on the drop-down arrow to the right of Operating System.

7. Select your operating system.

8. Click on the Find It! button.

9. Click on the Internet Explorer version you chose and follow the download instructions. At first, you'll only be getting a small setup wizard to manage your options selection and analyze your system.

10. Once downloading is complete, run the file, and follow the instructions. This is a big download (18 MB at last check) and it might take a couple of tries before you succeed. Or you can order the CD-ROM version online or via phone. If you have Windows 98, just click that little Update button on the Start Menu.

TIP: If you have Internet Explorer version 5 Beta, uninstall it. You won't be able to install the updated version correctly over the Beta version. To uninstall the Beta version::

1. Click on the Start button, Settings, and then Control Panel.

2. Click on the Add/Remove Programs icon.

3. Click on the Install/Uninstall tab.

4. Click on the Beta version.

5. Click on the Add/Remove button and follow the rest of the procedure.

Do you want Microsoft to install everything for you right from its web site? If so:

1. If you wish to install directly from the Internet, just follow the above instructions. (If you ordered the installation CD-ROM, double-click on the file called Setup.exe and forget about the Internet.)

2. If you want to download the program file to install later, you'll be given the choice of Install Minimal or Customize Your Browser.

3. Click Advanced.

4. Click Download Only. This will copy the large (18 MB at last check) installation file to your machine but will not run the installation program. You can do that yourself later.

TIP: I recommend the Download Only option. This way you can hang onto the file and reinstall later or transfer it to another machine. Your download comes with 90 days of free Microsoft support, so surf over and e-mail their staff with any problems you encounter. Keep detailed notes of the problems you find. It might take a day or two for a response from a technician. As with any technician, provide as much information as possible.

With Typical Install, you get Outlook Express, Windows Media Player, and Multimedia Enhancements. This requires 70 MB to install and 55 MB to run. If you don't have a good e-mail program, Outlook Express is probably worth trying. You'll definitely want the Windows Media Player and Multimedia Enhancements just to check out the latest cool stuff on the Internet. The rest you could probably do without.

If you have got to have it all, select Full Install. This requires a massive 111 MB of space to install and another 80 MB to run. We don't recommend it.

If you like to play it safe, try Minimal Install; this gives you nothing but the browser. You can always add more goodies later. This requires 45 MB to install and 26 MB to run.

TIP: One Advanced Option I recommend is to Prevent Setup from Associating File Types with Internet Explorer. If you already have another graphics viewer on your machine, this will prevent IE from taking sole responsibility for your graphics files. Read the options carefully before choosing. If your computer stalls, you can restart the setup process by running Ie5setup.exe again. The program will try to start again where it left off.

38. How do I transfer my bookmarks between Netscape Navigator and Internet Explorer 5.x (IE5)?

Do the following:

1. Open Internet Explorer.
2. Go to File in the drop-down menu.

3. Click Import/Export. This will start Microsoft's Import/Export Wizard, which will guide you through the rest of the process. (If you're moving from Netscape to IE5, IE5 may have already copied your Netscape Bookmarks into your favorites list. Look for a folder called "Imported Bookmarks.")

This wizard represents Microsoft's new friendly face. It actually does make sharing information between Netscape and IE5 easier. If you use both browsers routinely, we recommend the upgrade to IE5 for this reason alone.

Note that in browserspeak, "Bookmarks" are for Netscape and "Favorites" are for Microsoft. Don't let the names fool you; they're the same. No one cares about this except the software companies but understanding their lingo makes transferring between the two a little more clear.

TIP: When importing Bookmarks, IE5 will copy them over from Netscape without interfering with your current Favorites list; it asks where you would like to place the new Favorites in your current list. When exporting, say to another machine, you might have to save the Favorites as a file or overwrite your old Bookmarks. Bookmarks and Favorites are both .html links, which browsers can read as a web page from your hard drive. If you would rather not overwrite your old Bookmarks, make careful note of where you save your Bookmarks and what you choose to call the file. You can open this new file as a web page from any browser.

Your cookies can also be imported/exported using this command. Consider transferring cookies if you're computing on the road and like features that provide you with custom searches or instant news. Unlike Bookmarks/Favorites, cookies are simple text files. You could open them with any word processor, but why would you want to?

Netscape cookies are saved in one tidy little file called cookies.txt. Very handy if you want to copy or delete them all at once. Internet Explorer saves each cookie as its own text file under your Windows/Cookies/directory. Exporting cookies to Netscape means you'll have to either overwrite your entire cookies.txt file or do some tricky cutting and pasting. But importing cookies to Internet Explorer just means adding more files to your Cookies directory.

Definitions:

HyperText Markup Language (.HTML) file: Most simple web pages are text files with an .htm or .html extension after the file name. This identifies the file to your web browser as a web page, causing it to interpret the characters as HyperText Markup Language. Try opening an .html file on your hard drive with Windows Notepad and you'll see the basic text code.

Cookies: Cookies are simple text files created by a web site on your computer. They identify you as a specific visitor to a web site and are often used for the shopping cart or personal home page features offered by many sites. Contrary to popular belief, cookies are generic ID numbers; they store some of your actions online, but they don't store personal information. But if sites can tie your cookie to information you enter directly to a site (when ordering merchandise or registering software, for example), that information can be combined with your web-viewing habits and sold. Always use caution when entering personal information on any site that doesn't carefully state its privacy policy.

39. I downloaded a file from the Internet, but I can't open it. What should I do?

Look at the name of the file you have downloaded on your computer. Does it have an *extension*? The extension is the three or four characters after the last period in the file name. If none of your files appear to have extensions (they're just hidden) change your view settings as follows:

1. In Windows Explorer, click view from the menu.

2. Click Folder Options.

3. Examine the list for "hide extensions for known file types" and uncheck it.

4. Click OK.

If your file is still missing its extension, you will have to add one.

1. If you know the type of file then rename the file including the appropriate extension. Highlight the file.

2. Go to File and click Rename.

If you cannot guess the correct extension, contact the file's author for help.

If you have a file with an extension which you still cannot open you might not have the program required to open it. Try this:

1. Start one of your graphics or office applications.

2. Go to File, Open and attempt to access you file.

3. If that doesn't work try File, Import.

4. If none of this works then contact the file's author for help.

If you cannot find the file you have downloaded you can search for it, do the following:

1. Start one of your graphics or office applications.

2. Go to File, Open and attempt to access your file.

3. In the All Files dialog box enter the filename plus extension if you know it. If you don't know the extension you can replace it with an asterix.

4. In the Look In box select local hard drives.

5. Check the Include Subfolders button.

6. Click Find Now to start the search.

Definitions:

Extension: The characters after the last dot (period) in file names in Windows. Windows looks at the extension to decide which program to use to open the file. If the extension is missing or incorrect, Windows may not be able to decide which program to invoke.

40. I saved a web page but now it doesn't display properly. What do I do?

Some web pages are more complex than others. Those with special goodies might not run as expected because the images you see might have been generated on-the-fly by a script language within the page. Internet Explorer doesn't save the script when saving the page, so some images might come up missing. The error messages Explorer gives you won't help much.

To save the page in another way:

1. Open Internet Explorer.

2. Click on Favorites from the drop-down menu.

3. Click on Add to Favorites.

4. Check the box that says Make available offline.

When you use File, Save As, to save your page, IE assumes you want the page saved exactly as written. So always use Favorites to store pages you want to experience the way you first did. Use File, Save As, if you want the HTML code for another purpose later.

Definitions:

HyperText Markup Language (HTML): A language for writing web pages. Basic web pages can be written with any text editor, including Windows Notepad. Check your local library or the Internet for basic HTML primers.

Link: A special feature of HTML that you'll find on almost every web page. An object or line of text is used as a button with which to call another web page, e-mail program, etc. Each link refers to a line of HTML code containing a URL.

Uniform Resource Locator (URL): A path to a specific file on a computer network. URLs may point to files on your computer, on a local server, or on the Internet. The information in a URL directs HTML-compatible software to a new location or action. For example, URLs beginning with http:// indicate web pages.

41. I want to keep other users from visiting certain sites on the web.

First of all, what kind of information do you want to restrict? The obvious answer is pornography, but you might want to restrict access to other sorts of material on your machine. Microsoft Internet Explorer version 5 (IE5) comes with tools to help you manage restrictions in various ways:

1. Click on the Start button, Settings, Control and then the Internet icon.

2. Click on Content.

3. Click Enable.

4. Click on the Approved Sites tab.

5. Enter the Uniform Resource Locators (URLs) of any sites you want to restrict access to. Unlike filtering systems based on language, this is absolute. The URL is the unique property of a web site. So unless the URL changes (which can happen), the site is off limits.

6. Click Ratings. Your browser either responds to sites that rate themselves or checks with the Ratings authors to see how they rate this site. But if the site is unrated (as a lot of harmless sites might be), you're not allowed to proceed.

7. If you want to be able to override the limits with a password, check the box. If you want to disable the Content Advisor, back out to the Content tab and click Disable. If you have set up a

password, you'll need to enter it here. Make sure to keep a record of your password somewhere safe.

TIP: You can amend or adjust your Ratings system by clicking the Advanced tab. Here you can choose alternate ratings systems from different organizations online and also some different rules-based filtering protocols that can be applied to all sites. Some of these organizations might use philosophies that closely match your own and don't screen out material you might consider benign.

NOTE: If you click on Control Panel, Internet Options, Content, General, you'll notice a couple of useful check boxes. Check Allow Users to See Unrated Sites if you get sick of being constantly filtered out for not having a rating. But a lot of sites are unrated, so you're taking a risk.

Definitions:

Rules-based filtering protocol: Standards for keeping sites from reaching your computer. Filtering protocols generally take one of two approaches. Some rely on lists of pre-screened sites to allow or disallow. Others rely on basic rules that are applied to each site as you visit. Rules-based filters can catch new or changing sites that list-based filters might miss. However, rules can't cover every situation; some good sites might be filtered out while a few bad ones get through.

42. Should I worry about cookies?

Probably not. Most cookies are for your convenience, allowing automatic logons to your favorite sites or storing items in your virtual shopping cart while you browse.

If cookies bug you, you can disable them:

1. Open Internet Explorer.

2. Click on View from the drop-down menu.

3. Click on Internet Options.

    4. Click on the Advanced tab.

    5. Select the limiting functions within this area.

CAUTION: Be warned that if you limit cookies, you'll spend a lot more time clicking yes or no than browsing. Cookies only store information, and sometimes are not used at all by the web site (a lot of web site software creates cookies by default). They can only be used by the site that created them and they can't read information about your system and send it back. A cookie can only track you on your visit to that particular site.

However, cookies can give companies a window onto your web habits. If you visit a site that deposits a cookie on your computer, that site is assigning you a unique ID number. When you return, the site recognizes your ID number and records which links you click on and which terms you search for. The site doesn't know your name until you enter it on the site.

When you order merchandise or register for a contest, the site can tie your personal information to your cookie ID number. The site now has a very valuable database entry on you which includes any information you enter plus the things you like to do while visiting this site. If enough sites buy and sell enough of these records, eventually companies can get a very thorough picture of you. Read web site privacy policies carefully and avoid entering any personal information whenever possible. The danger with cookies is not crime but advertising.

43. I want to save part of this web page. How do I do this?

Do you want to save the entire page?

    1. See question 44.

Do you want to save just a portion of the displayed text?The easiest way is with the Clipboard:

    1. Highlight what you want as you would with a word processor.

    2. Click on Edit from the drop-down menu.

    3. Click on Copy. This copies the selection to the Clipboard.

4. Open a document in another application.

5. Click on Edit from the drop-down menu.

6. Click on Paste. This inserts your item into the second application.

Do you want to drag and drop the item directly into a document?

1. Carefully highlight the item you want, just as you would in a word processor. With the target document open in its own window, click and hold the left mouse button over the highlighted item and drag it onto its new location.

Do you want to copy an image?

1. Right-click on the image you want.

2. Click Save Picture As.

Do you want to save the image as your desktop background?

1. Right-click the image.

2. Click Set as Wallpaper.

Definitions:

Clipboard: An application that comes with Microsoft Windows helping you to move text or graphics from one document to another. When you use the Copy, Cut, or Paste commands, you're transferring information to and from the Windows Clipboard. You can actually see what is currently on your Clipboard with the Clipboard Viewer. You can find this program on the Start Menu under Programs, Accessories, System Tools.

44. I want to save a whole web page on my computer. How do I do this?

1. Go to File in the drop-down menu.

2. Click on Save As.

3. In the Save In box, select a location for all the files that make up the page. Explorer will save the basic page code plus any images included with the page as separate files in the location you specify.

4. If the option in the Save As Type box reads "Web Page, complete," Internet Explorer saves the whole page with all its separate graphics files, frames, etc., each complete in its own format. If you open the .html file that belongs to this group from your hard drive, all the images will appear intact.

If you have installed Outlook Express 5 or higher (which comes with Internet Explorer), you also have a really cool option: When saving, select Web Archive in the Save As Type box and the page will be saved as it appears in your browser in a single tidy file that can be e-mailed as an attachment.

If you just want the page source code:

1. Select Web Page, HTML only. This doesn't save related graphics and such, but it will invoke Internet Explorer when opened.

2. Select Text Only. This saves just the visible text on a web page to a simple .txt file.

TIP: If you would like easy access to the page from a document or your desktop, without saving all the information in the page, create a Shortcut. The easiest way is to browse to the page in Internet Explorer, then look in the Address bar. There will be a small Internet Explorer icon right next to the address. Drag this icon to the desktop or an open document and a shortcut will appear that points to the page location on the Internet.

45. I want to print this web page. How do I do this?

Do the following:

1. Go to File and then Page Setup.

2. Check to see that your page size and margins are as you would like them.

3. Go to File, Print and, if necessary, select Properties to adjust options specific to your printer.

TIP: If you're viewing a page with frames, the Print Frames portion of the Print dialog will become active. This can be useful if you want to print the real content of a frames page without the ads, buttons, indexes, credits, etc.

46. Can ActiveX or Java programs harm my system by running from the Internet?

ActiveX Controls provide a potential port of entry to your computer for malicious or poorly written applications. Under default security settings, Microsoft uses Authenticode to check the digital signature embedded in an ActiveX Controls code. You must understand, though, that ActiveX Controls are programs that Internet Explorer can download, install, and run without your supervision. Security settings are the only way to limit your risk from this type of software. Internet Explorer's default settings are generally appropriate, but if you haven't checked them recently, open them up and confirm that they are as they should be.

Java Applets are like ActiveX Controls in that they are programs that Internet Explorer can download, install, and run to provide extra features on web pages. The big difference is that Java Applets run from within a virtual machine set up on your computer. This provides a strictly controlled environment. The downside is that these programs don't have the freedom to interact with files and other programs. Also, Java Applets don't store themselves on your hard drive. When their job is done, they delete themselves and so must be downloaded each time your browser encounters them on the Web. You can limit Java's role on your machine much like you can limit ActiveX but the options don't provide much added security for normal Internet usage:

1. Open Internet Explorer.

2. Click on Tools from the drop-down menu.

3. Click on Internet Options.

4. Check the Security tab.

5. Set the Internet Zone to Medium or higher. With these settings, ActiveX or Java programs are carefully limited.

Definitions:

Digital signature: A feature that relies on encryption to generate a unique identifying code. A recipient's computer can verify that the code was generated by the authentic user. Much of this process goes on behind the scenes in traffic to and from secure web sites.

47. How can I make sure that my web transactions are secure?

It is only safe to send vital data over the Internet if you're connected via a security protocol called Secure Sockets Layer (SSL). SSL connections start with the prefix https://. You'll be warned whenever you enter or leave an SSL site. All information passed to and from the site and your machine is encrypted. Only the secure site and your computer can decode the information transferred.

Perhaps the only stumbling block is the method of encryption. The National Security Administration (NSA) will not allow heavy-duty encryption software to be distributed outside the United States or Canada. Therefore, most Internet Explorer installations use the export version, which uses a weaker 40-bit encryption.

To check your version:

1. Open Windows Explorer.

2. Click on Tools from the drop-down menu.

3. Click on Find and then Files or Folders.

4. Type schannel.dll in the Named text box area.

5. Make sure the hard drive is selected in the Look In text box area.

6. Make sure you've checked the Include Subfolders checkbox. (You should find this file in the Windows folder.)

7. Click on the file.

8. Right-click on the file and select Properties. The Version tab will show Export Version if you have the 40-bit encryption and U.S. and Canada Version if you have the 128-bit encryption. Switching is a small upgrade, and well worth your time.

9. Go to *http://www.microsoft.com/ie* to download the upgrade.

Web transactions can challenge your security in two ways:

- Others can send messages posing as you.

- Web sites can look legitimate but really be bait to collect your personal information.

Internet Explorer provides methods to help assure you that neither can happen. These methods are based on public key cryptography. A web site certificate guarantees that a specific site is genuine. No other web site can assume the identity of a site protected by such a certificate. When you visit a secure site, Internet Explorer automatically downloads its certificate. Information your computer sends can then be decrypted only by the authentic web site owner.

Some sites may require proof of your identity before accepting information from you. As you might expect, this requires you to have your own personal certificate. You'll need to know which certification authority the site prefers so that you can obtain an acceptable personal certificate.

For buying online, a special personal certificate can be obtained from Visa and MasterCard conforming to the SET Protocol. This verifies that you're who you say you are and that you're authorized to use the credit card you're submitting.

Definitions:

Certificate: A certificate is a variation of a public key. Certificates are issued by widely trusted Certification Authorities. Once convinced of your identity, they will (for a small fee) issue a certificate for you or your business.

Public key cryptography: A method of encrypting sensitive information to prevent a thief from using it. An individual or company uses encryption software to generate a pair of "keys." The keys are really complex strings of characters: one is distributed to anyone who wants to send you information (the public key), and the other is kept safely on your computer (the private key). The sender must use your public key to encrypt information intended for you. Only the holder of the corresponding private key can decrypt the information.

48. How can I protect my computer when downloading files from the Internet?

You can limit your vulnerability when downloading files in a variety of ways. Use your Internet Options to change how Internet Explorer behaves in different security situations.

1. Open Internet Explorer

2. Click on Tools from the drop-down menu.

3. Click on Internet Options.

4. Click on the Security tab.

5. Use the slider to adjust the security level for each Zone shown. Read the descriptions of each level for more details.

NOTE: Keep in mind the following:

• High security disables your ability to download files and cookies, which can be frustrating. High security also disables all ActiveX Controls, regardless of their source.

• Medium security prompts you before downloading most content. It also enables cookies. Authenticode is used to verify the authenticity of ActiveX Controls before and allowing them to run.

• Medium-Low security is the same as Medium but without the prompts.

- Low security accepts all content and programs without verifying their sources, which can be risky.

I recommend the default settings for each zone. Click the Default Level button to reset each zone to Microsoft standard settings.

Definitions:

ActiveX Control: Programs that Internet Explorer can download, install, and run without the user's supervision. These programs can give web pages a lot of extra functionality. They differ from other active content on the Internet in that they can interact directly with your computer's files and other programs.

Authenticode: A Microsoft approach to automating security on the web. When you're browsing, Internet Explorer looks at your Security settings and takes precautions appropriate to the type of sites you're visiting. Many sites can verify their identity by using certificates, which Authenticode can automatically download and check. If a certificate appears invalid, Authenticode will alert you and prompt you for further action.

Zones: Microsoft categorizes different destinations in the networked world by Zone. The Local Intranet Zone represents your specific machine and others connected to you on a private network. The Internet Zone represents computers on outside networks such as the web. Trusted Sites are sites specifically designated by you as safe. Restricted Sites are sites designated by you as particularly dangerous.

49. How do I find a page I visited in the past?

How long has it been?

1. A few days ago? Click the History button to access the History bar. You can select the approximate range of time within which you think you were last at the desired site. Click on the page icon you want to return to.

2. One of the last nine pages? Click the little triangle just to the right of the Back button. This will display a drop down list of the last nine pages viewed. Click the one you want.

3. Mere seconds ago? Hit the Back button to retrace your steps. (Alt+Left Arrow works as well.)

TIP: You can change the number of days stored in the History list. To do this:

1. Click on Tools from the drop-down menu.

2. Click on Internet Options.

3. Click the General tab. At the bottom, you'll see a place to specify the length of time to keep entries in your History log.

NOTE: Windows 95 and Windows 98 may also be set to clear the History bar each time you quit or start Windows. If your History bar seems to be empty every time you try it, check Control Panel for a Tweak UI option. If the Tweak UI icon is present, it may be set to clean out your History. Double-click the icon and click the Paranoia tab to see your current settings.

50. How do I send an e-mail. How do I do this?

Since you have Internet Explorer installed you probably also have Outlook Express, the free little brother of Microsoft Outlook. (If you have Outlook, the steps shown below should still apply.) Outlook provides additional features for managing personal information but its e-mail functions are very similar to those in Outlook Express.

TIP: To avoid confusion, if you have Microsoft Outlook on your computer, use it exclusively to send and receive e-mail. Outlook Express will send and receive independently and doesn't offer many of Outlook's valuable functions.

Do you have Outlook Express on your system?

1. Go to your Start menu and look for an icon for Outlook Express. Chances are that if you bought a computer with Windows 95 or later preinstalled, Internet Explorer and Outlook Express are on it.

If you don't have Outlook Express, you'll need to reinstall Internet Explorer to get it. See question 37. Then:

1. In Outlook Express click on Tools, Accounts, and Mail tab.

2. Click Add, Mail to set up a new e-mail account.

3. Follow the instructions on each screen. You'll need the specific names of your mail servers, as well as your user name and password. Contact your Internet Service Provider for help.

So, now you have Outlook Express. To send an e-mail:

1. Click on the Outlook Express icon.

2. Click on File, New, and then Mail Message. A new window should appear with boxes for the recipient's e-mail address, subject, etc.

3. Type the recipient's e-mail address into the To: box. Be precise and always use all lowercase letters. An Internet e-mail address will be in the format username@server.xyz. A local network e-mail address might just include the username.

TIP: If you have addresses stored in your Microsoft Address Book, click on the small icon to the left of the To: box. This will allow you to choose a recipient from your Address Book

4. Type a description of your message in the Subject line. People may consider you rude to send an e-mail without a subject.

5. Type your message in the large window below.

6. When finished, click Send. This should queue your message in the Outbox to be sent later. In order to complete the sending process, click Send/Receive. (To see what messages are in your Outbox waiting to be sent, check the list of folders on the left of your Outlook Express window. If the folder labeled Outbox is bold, messages are inside waiting to be sent with Send/Receive. Double-click on the Outbox to view its contents.)

7. Verify that your message has been sent by double-clicking the Sent Items folder. By default, sent messages are saved here.

If you have new e-mail, the folder labeled Inbox will appear bold. Double-click it to view your messages. Unread messages appear in bold.

51. I like Internet Explorer version 5.x (IE5), but I do not need a lot of the special features. How do I get rid of them?

Microsoft lets you remove the ones you do not need without messing up your browser:

1. Click on the Start button, Settings, Control Panel, and then the Add/Remove Programs icon.

2. Click on Install/Uninstall.

3. Click on Remove Selected Components. This will put you into "maintenance mode." Follow the prompts to restore your system to its pre-IE5 condition.

If you have had enough of IE5 altogether, see question 52 or, update your version if that helps.

TIP: I recommend leaving Media Player on your system. This is a handy movie viewer to keep installed and updated, even without Internet Explorer.

52. Internet Explorer is malfunctioning. Can I fix it? Can I uninstall it?

Microsoft packages IE5 with some tools to make it easier to make things right:

1. Click on the Start button, Settings, Control Panel, and then the Add/Remove Programs icon.

2. Click on Install/Uninstall.

3. Click Repair. This will attempt to locate corrupted files critical to IE5 and replace them. Follow the prompts. If this doesn't work, consider uninstalling IE5 and reinstalling it from scratch. (You'll need the big installation file; either you already have it, or you'll need to reinstall from the Microsoft web site.)

4. Click Restore the previous Windows configuration. This will put you into "maintenance mode." Follow the prompts to restore your system to its pre-IE condition.

TIP: You may run into some "problems" with other Microsoft programs when you uninstall Internet Explorer. Most of them are related to importing/exporting web pages and direct access to e-mail programs from within products like Microsoft Office. Generally, all these situations are easily overcome by transferring files to other browser or e-mail programs.

You may encounter some odd behavior after uninstalling IE5. As a "fix," Microsoft recommends (drumroll, please) reinstalling IE5. You might instead try uninstalling/reinstalling the program that's giving you trouble. If none of this works, restart your computer in "Safe Mode".

To restart in Safe Mode:

1. Shut down your computer completely.

2. Restart your computer.

3. Hold down the F8 button before your computer completely reboots if you have Windows 95; or, hold down the Control (Ctrl) button if you have Windows 98.

4. Choose Safe Mode from the startup menu which appears.

5. Reinstall IE5 (see question 37).

6. Uninstall IE5. Keep track of every step you do here in case you need to call tech support.

E-BUSINESS

What exactly is e-business? Many people talk about it, but, as with most buzzwords, few understand what it really means.

E-business is a way of doing business using a collection of technology-based applications to automate transactions and exchange information.

It has three core areas:

- E-business sites

- Applications used to automate the process and bandwidth (the speed at which your organization communications to the outside world)

- Security (how your organization is protected from the outside world)

Because each topic in itself could make up its own book, we will examine only some of the more common basic issues.

53. When an organization conducts e-business, with whom is it doing business?

There are many different subsets for e-business, but they can generally be grouped into three main categories:

- *E-commerce* uses technology to facilitate online transactions using credit cards, approved credit, cyber bucks and other ways to purchase things over the Internet.

- *Business-to-consumer (B2C) e-business* refers to online marketing to consumers over the Internet.

- *Business-to-business (B2B) e-business* is a technology-based system made up of applications and local and wide area networks (LANs and WANs) to automate the ways business partners work with each other.

54. How should an e-business system be implemented?

If you want to do business on the Internet:

- Identify your business objectives.

- Devise a solid system of measuring whether you've met them.

- Define your business processes and procedures. Many organizations don't have these in place. To implement e-business and understand your Return On Investment (ROI), this is a must.

- Analyze how e-business will impact your organization, your customers, and your business partners.

- Research which technologies will make your organization better, and how they should be implemented. Simply throwing a technology at a problem will not fix it.

- Make sure your e-business system can grow with your needs. Don't buy a big system that you can grow into; instead, consider a system that fits your existing needs and can be scaled up to accommodate growth.

- Implement a security system. In most organizations, hackers are a minor threat to the organization; the main culprits are disgruntled former employees or business partners working for your competitors. Arrange to monitor user activity as well as protect valuable intellectual property.

E-Business can make a company more agile in reacting to market trends, improve the logistics of information and communication, help to clean up some poorly implemented business procedures, and reduce management and logistic costs. But only if it's done carefully.

55. What are some of the applications that make up e-business?

Here are just a few:

- *Enterprise resource planning applications (ERP):* Organizations use an ERP application to run their e-business program.

- *Marketing automation encompasses* a group of technologies for serving the customer and helping to drive sales.

- *Sales and customer service automation* is an assortment of applications allowing the sales force to manage and maintain customer relationships.

- *Data warehousing* is a search tool that uncovers non-obvious patterns and indicators in an organization's business conditions.

- *Distributed training* uses technology to deliver interactive, video-based training over a network. Also called distance learning.

- *Call centers* integrate an organization's telephone relations with telephony (voice, voicemail, faxes) and computer technology, including the web.

- *E-mail programs* send and receive messages and transfer files, applications, and even faxes.

56. What are the most common types of applications used for e-business?

Other than e-mail, the applications that most companies are implementing are:

- Enterprise resource planning (ERP) applications

- Marketing automation

- Sales and customer service automation

Enterprise Resource Planning (ERP) Systems

ERP systems are a lot like the Microsoft office suite (Word, Excel, PowerPoint, Access, and Outlook), with more than one program and able to do a variety of things. You personally may not use all the programs, but the organization probably will. And they usually don't do everything you want them to, so you may have to add other programs or customize an application that can work with these programs to better suit your needs.

57. How does an ERP system run a business?

ERP systems:

- Provide a technology-derived architecture based on software that integrates a diverse range of business processes.

- Help companies to be more responsive to changing markets and deliver better service at lower cost.

- Usually require a significant or complete overhaul of the organization's IT infrastructure.

- Can help an organization clean up bad habits by forcing employees to all follow defined procedures.

- Require you to examine your organization's network bandwidth so that information reaches its designated location as quickly as possible, thereby improving efficiency.

- Offer modules for finance, transportation, service, manufacturing, and distribution.

- May also make it possible for your organization to integrate business with external suppliers, partners, and even customers.

- May allow you to use a bar code system to track parts, inventory, and finished products.

58. What should be taken into consideration when implementing an ERP program?

Think about:

- The types of functions you want to include in the system. These are generally grouped into five areas: finance, manufacturing, logistics, sales, and HR/payroll.

- The more functions you implement, the more complex and costly your system will become; in overall outlay and maintenance.

- The size of your organization and the user population will make a difference.

- User interaction: There are two types of users, those who have heavy interaction with the system, and casual users.

- The system's complexity will increase proportionately with the percentage of heavy users.

- Organization geography: Factor in the total number of servers you'll need and where they'll be located—a single location or multiple locations?

- Single-site deployments are the simplest; multiple-site configurations are highly complex.

- Do you have legacy systems? Are they up to date? How much time will it take to integrate or prep these systems to interface with your ERP packages?

- Ask how well an off-the-shelf package would work with your organization; try not to over-customize the system. An ERP program works best, especially when it's an upgrade to the system, when it has fewer customizations.

Marketing Automation

Marketing automation allows an organization to develop close ties with its clients, whether B2B or B2C. Implementing these projects requires a centralized data solution—such as customer databases with order history and shipping information—to allow the organization to understand what a customer wants, has ordered, and has experienced with orders. Knowing this, business can identify and track customer trends, better understand customer needs, and change business practices to meet the needs, which translates to greater customer loyalty.

59. What functions can benefit from marketing automation?

These are the most obvious:

- Lead management, marketing campaign execution, and print collateral management.

- Demographic analysis, variable segmentation, and customer buying and shopping habits.

- Cross-channel marketing, telesales, telemarketing, direct mail, fax, e-mail, and web.

- Identifying existing customers and differentiating them from non-customers. This allows you to develop marketing programs targeted to each audience.

- Identifying cross-selling and up-selling opportunities, and promoting one-to-one marketing where you personalize the customer experience.

60. How is a business-to-customer (B2C) marketing campaign implemented?

Usually, a B2C campaign:

- Targets industries such as retail, finance, and other consumer-oriented services.

- Provides customer tracking.

- Requires databases attached to the site that can contain customer profiles. Large marketing campaigns usually require a legacy system for support.

61. How is a web marketing campaign implemented?

A web campaign usually:

- Can use the Internet (e-mail or Web) as the marketing delivery system.

- Can be integrated into a direct mail, fax, or telephone campaign.

- Targets customers who are typically in the organization's e-mail directory.

- Includes mass e-mailings (with embedded URLs or links to a targeted site).

- Uses cookies or other tracking systems to measure the effectiveness of the campaign and track the habits of the buying audience.

62. How can we best analyze our web marketing data?

Just as with other marketing campaigns:

- Set sound, realistic objectives.

- Chart activity against your objectives; if possible, relate it to data contained in your ERP.

- Use web server analysis that allows you to track types of browsers and platforms. This information can be good to know if you are new applications that may be browser or platform specific.

- Measure all data to plot trends. If the campaign is extremely large, you may need a data mining application to understand any non-obvious trends.

Sales Force and Customer Service Automation

Whether out of town or just out of the office, your sales force needs to be in touch with the organization. Sales force automation is a group of technologies that keeps salespeople in touch with clients and associates. These technologies use a centralized system to track customers, orders, and incidents. This allows for better service to clients and customers.

63. How is sales force automation implemented?

There are many ways. For instance,

- Equipped with laptop computers and remote network access, salespeople in the field can immediately access necessary information, such as meeting schedules, sales reports, customer data, delivery dates, order status, and presentations.

- This allows them to increase their ability to close the deal and support the client.

- Applications include contact managers and planners, order tracking, and on-line presentations.

- Some systems include order management and fulfillment, and lead generation and tracking.

Before implementing sales force automation examine the basic computing needs of the sales force, costs of laptop computer for all reps, remote dial-up services, and which applications will be needed:

- Perform a realistic ROI analysis so that you can better understand the purpose of your investment.

- Examine alternatives when possible, such as Palm Pilots instead of laptops, and DSL or cable modems for remote branch offices.

64. How do Customer Service Centers (CSC) work?

These call centers:

- Mainly consist of post-sales activities, though field and plant areas are sometimes part of the system.

- Generally, provide support for defective or broken products, incomplete or inaccurate orders, and other service-related issues.

- Usually must communicate with many other areas of the company, including sales, marketing, manufacturing, and accounting.

- Must be able to access all areas that are vital to customer service.

- Require several different software packages to create a workable CSC platform for most organizations.

- Require integrated marketing automation, sales tracking, customer service, ERP, and other e-business systems.

SECURITY AND FIREWALLS

With the advent of damaging viruses like *I Love You* and *Melissa*, network security has been a major concern for most organizations. Hacker attacks have brought down major government (Army and CIA) and commercial sites (eBay and Yahoo!). Organizations are constantly surprised by how little time viruses or hackers need to hit their targets. Yet, in most cases, a closely monitored security system can prevent an intruder from penetrating a network.

65. How does an Internet firewall work?

A firewall is a computer system or group of systems that polices traffic between an organization's internal network and the external Internet. It regulates who from the outside may enter the system, and what network services they may access. To be effective, a firewall:

- Should incorporate packet filtering so that all traffic to and from the Internet must pass through the firewall.

- Permit only authorized traffic to enter your network.

- Limit network access to those inside the organization, and restrict employee access to web sites or prevent them from browsing at all.

Once an intruder has gotten past the firewall your defenses are broken and the whole network is exposed. A firewall must, therefore, be part of an overall security program that includes corporate confidentiality policies, virus protection, user authentication, and log-in access. A system administrator can employ a proxy service to determine what network services and features are available to which employees.

66. What are the benefits of an Internet firewall?

With a firewall, system administrators can:

- Audit network usage, such as tracking what sites employees are visiting and even pinpointing who went there.

- Identify network bottlenecks.

- Audit log files to see if files have been compromised.

- Use a bastion host to protect against intruders and hackers.

The firewall creates a single point of failure so that if the Internet connection is interrupted, the internal network will continue to perform without any problems.

67. What are some of the things a firewall can't protect against?

Here are a few:

- Disgruntled employees instigating corporate espionage.

- Information copied onto floppy disks or other removable media, laptops, or any other computer information that leaves the corporate environment other than through the network.

- Hackers or thieves who have stolen passwords.

- Systems where the general default login configurations are not changed.

- Information that is purposely sent *out* via e-mail.

- Viruses contained within e-mail attachments (an anti-virus program needs to be implemented to catch this).

- Back doors, which are unpublished entry points in a system.

Definitions:

Back door: A security hole in a system that allows continued access to the system by an intruder even if the original attack is discovered.

Bastion host: An Internet firewall system specifically designed to protect against intruders.

Internet firewall: A system or group of systems that enforces an access control policy between an organization's network and the Internet.

Packet filtering: A feature that allows a router to make a permit/deny decision for each packet based on the packet header information made available to the IP forwarding process.

Proxy service: A special-purpose, application-level code installed on an Internet firewall gateway to allow the network administrator to permit or deny specific applications or specific features of an application.

Comparing Telephone Services

Connecting your office or remote sites to the Internet usually requires a high-speed phone connection. However, choosing one is not easy. Here are some of the most common high-speed, telecommunications service options:

- Analog phone lines

- Switched 56

- X.25

- Point-to-point dedicated leased lines

- Frame relay

- xDSL (including ADSL, IDSL and others)

- Cable

- SMDS

- ISDN

- ATM

68. Which type of phone service is best for our Internet network connection?

Since organization size, needs, and network configurations vary, along with telecommunications rates across the country, it is impossible for us to answer this question. With that in mind, what follows should be used as a basis for identifying the services that best fit your organization.

We also recommend that you stick with a broad-band service, like xDSL, and cable modems because they typically offer the best price to performance ratio.

Definitions:

Analog Lines: Analog lines, sometimes referred to at POTS (plain old telephone service), have been around since the telephone first came into homes and businesses. POTS lines, like the old record albums, at the time of their development were optimized to carry voice communications, not modern digital communications (like computers or compact disks). POTS lines are most useful when digital lines are not available or too expensive. Top data rate for analog lines is 56K, but more users don't achieve these speeds even with a 56K modem. Therefore, analog lines are not a good option for supporting network data.

Switched 56 Lines: In some areas that lack newer digital service or can't afford it, switched 56 can be a good low-cost option. It's like analog service except that it's digital and used to support data-only services at rates of 56 Kbps. However, given its low bandwidth, many service providers have raised the price to deter customers in favor of faster, high-speed networks. Therefore may not be available in all areas.

Point-to-Point Dedicated Leased Lines: Many companies still use private leased lines, which run at speeds ranging from 56 Kbps to 1.544 Mbps (T1 speeds). These high-speed point-to-point connections are used where security is a major concern. These types of connections are paid for by tariffs, which are based on connection speeds and the distance between locations. Given the wide range of current options and Internet technologies, organizations should consider other options first.

Frame Relay: Frame relay is based on standards defined by ANSI, with speeds ranging from 56/64 Kbps to 1.544 Mbps. It's currently used in many remote enterprise connections because of its ability to provide bandwidth when needed, and it can handle sudden bursts of traffic, such as large file transfers, over long distances. Unfortunately, Frame relay can be up to ten times more expensive than comparable technology and requires dedicated access lines.

Digital Subscriber Line (DSL): DSL is a technology that brings high-bandwidth connectivity to homes and small businesses using standard POTS phone lines. (xDSL refers to the family of digital subscriber line technologies, such as ADSL, HDSL, and RADSL.) Connection speeds for DSL can range from 1.544 Mbps to 512 Kbps downstream (receiving data) and around 128 Kbps upstream (sending data). DSL uses one line to carry both voice and data signals, and the data connection is consistently connected to your Internet Service Provider (ISP), maintaining a constant connection. The DSL standard is supported by ANSI (American National Standards Institute).

Cable Service: The cable industry has been adding an Internet-ready network to provide services beyond traditional broadcast TV. Cable modems attach to the cable TV network connection, eliminating the dialup process required for analog modems. These networks support file transfer rates from 500 Kbps to 30 Mbps. The major disadvantage with a cable network is that it is shared. This means that if your neighbor is doing data-intensive work, such as downloading many huge files, your connection will slow to a crawl. Cable companies, aware of this problem, have developed a networking model that would connect smaller groups of people and eliminate the data transfer problems.

Cable modems are designed to meet the growing demands of residential computer users, who want faster Internet access, use interactive TV, or telecommute to work. The advantage is that these services don't require dial-in modems.

Integrated Services Digital Network (ISDN): ISDN was originally expected to replace POTS. It provides two channels, each running at 64Kbps that can be combined for a total throughput of 128Kbps. In addition, ISDN provides two phone numbers so that you can use the same ISDN line to make voice calls while still being connected to the network. However, unlike DSL, your computer connection will drop from the full 128Kbps to the single channel rate of 64Kbps. For ISDN, the phone company must install new digital services in their phone switches to support the digitally switched connection. In addition, ISDN is generally more expensive than DSL and equipment costs are generally higher.

Asynchronous Transfer Mode (ATM): ATM operates at speeds from 1.544 Mbps to 622 Mbps. It's a high-speed network protocol that breaks down large data files into smaller files to more them quickly. In a sense, it works like this: If you have a train in San Diego that has a mile of cars and it is going to Buffalo, ATM will send each car on a separate route at higher speeds because a smaller train is faster. On reaching Buffalo, all cars will be reassembled in the exact previous order. Because it can break down large files, ATM works best with real-time voice, data, images, and video.

69. What factors should I take into consideration to decide which telecommunications standard to adopt?

These are some of the most important:

- Estimate service charges, installation, monthly service cost, and other overall usage costs.

- Estimate the cost of equipment you'll need to support the communications technology, including hardware, cabling, maintenance, and support.

- Define what server-level software each service requires, including network management, security, and protocols to be supported.

- Estimate support costs, including installation, training, frequency and planned extensions and changes, and troubleshooting.

- Estimate network management costs, including ease of corrections or moves, and network extensions and changes.

- Decide what types of data you will be transferring: video, text, files, graphics?

70. Our organization had a high-speed digital network installed as part of our initiative to provide Internet access to our employees. But over the past few months, it really seems slow. Why? Do we need a faster Internet connection?

A slowdown occurs for many reasons. To check them out:

- Use network-monitoring software to gauge network performance. Often things feel faster when they're new; as you get used to them over time, they don't seem that fast.

- If you did your homework in selecting your network connection, you probably don't need to upgrade your speed, unless you increased your staff.

- Another possibility is that people have gotten used to sending files around the office via e-mail. Often it would be better to put files in a network directory; use e-mail to tell other people where to find the files.

- Computer networks are like roads. If you fill them with packets (the computer equivalent of a car), your network will slow down. So, if you often send large graphic files to your associates, you're creating a great deal of traffic. See the point immediately above.

- Corporate logos, presentations, and other material that may be used are best placed in a network directory where individuals can access them when needed.

71. For a small business or a home office, DSL and cable seem like good options. What are their differences?

DSL is currently the better technology, but it is in its early days. Also, since there is such diversity in services, a lot depends on where you are. But these are the basic differences between DSL and Internet cable services:

DSL:

- Is offered by telephone companies and provides a wide variety of service options.

- Gives you a single line that allows you to talk on the phone and use the Internet at the same time.

- Has service levels that can be adjusted by the phone companies where demand is high. This prevents network slowdown by one subscriber using a lot of bandwidth; in the future, it may better accommodate interactive TV, streaming video, and music on demand services.

- Is designed to provide two channels, upstream and downstream, for sending and receiving.

Cable:

- Is offered by cable companies, which means that, in most areas, users are limited to a single service provider.

- Does not require a dial-up modem or connection to a telephone company because it uses existing cable TV lines.

- May be tied to a required cable TV subscription in addition to Internet access.

- Uses a shared network, so that the more people are using it, the slower your service. (The effect can be like someone flushing the toilet while you're in the shower.)

- Is designed as a single channel for sending a signal (down-stream). An additional channel or a second cable plant for upstream communications must be added before it can receive data commands from users.

Definitions:

American National Standards Institute (ANSI): An organization that sets widely recognized standards.

Asymmetric Digital Subscriber Line (ADSL): *See* xDSL.

Asynchronous Transfer Mode (ATM): A high-speed switching technology that uses 53-byte fixed-length cells to transmit data, voice, and video over networks.

Bps: Bits per second, a standard for data transmissions used to measure serial ports and modems.

Broadband: General term describing network service that transmits data at high rates.

Downstream: A term that describes downloading information from a network.

Frame Relay: A fast packet-switching technology for interconnecting Local Area Networks (LANs) at high speeds; the interface between user equipment and the Wide Area Network (WAN). It does not define internal operation of the network or the interface or protocols.

High-bit-rate Digital Subscriber Line (HDSL): *See* xDSL.

Integrated Services Digital Network (ISDN): ISDN is a public switched digital network that provides a wide variety of communications services and integrated access to the network.

Kbps: Kilobits per second with a transfer rate of 1,024 bytes per second.

Mbps: Megabits per second with a transfer rate of a million bits per second (1,048,576 bytes).

Plain Old Telephone Service (POTS): The existing analog telephone lines.

Single-line Digital Subscriber Line (SDSL): *See* xDSL.

Switched 56: Digital service that transmits data at speeds of 56 Kbps over circuit-switched telephone networks.

Telco: Common abbreviation for "telephone company."

Very-high-bit-rate Digital Subscriber Line (VDSL): *See* xDSL.

Wide Area Network (WAN): A network parts of which are in two separate physical locations.

Upstream: Term used to describe uploading information over a network

xDSL: Digital subscriber line technologies—ADSL, HDSL/SDSL, VDSL—that use twisted copper pairs to support broadband transmission rates.

Comparing Connections

	Analog Dial-Up	Switched 56	Point-to-Point Leased Lines	Frame Relay	xDSL	Cable	ISDN	T-1, ATM/ Broadband ISDN
Data Speed	9.6-56 Kbps data (33.6 Kbps is average connection rate)	56 Kbps data	1.544- 2.048 Mbps data	64 Kbps-1.544 Mbps	380Kbps-1.544-2.0 Mbps (depending on DSL variety)	500 Kbps-30 Mbps	64-128 Kbps for BRI voice, video, and data 1.544-2.0 Mbps for PRI voice, video, and data	1.544 Mbps-622 Mbps voice, video, and data (25-155 Mbps typical)
Uses	Voice and data on separate lines	Voice and data on separate lines	High speed voice and data	High speed data from Point-to-point locations	• Internet access • Video (TV) • Video conference • Video on demand • Remote LAN access	• Internet access • Video (TV) • Video conference • Video on demand • Remote LAN access	Voice, data, and video on a single digital line	• Voice • Data • Video
Benefits	• Wide availability • Low cost	• Wide availability • Moderate cost • Uses standard telephone numbers	• High speed reliable • Security • Direct connections to Internet	High speed bandwidth-on-demand point-to-point connectivity	Broadband bandwidth, simultaneous digital services and lifeline POTS, dedicated (not shared), supports multimedia service	Hight speed existing infrastructure, fast call setup	High speed; digital data, voice, images, video on integrated line; fast call setup; secure, reliable, stable digital connectivity; efficient for bursty traffic; standardized protocols	Very high speed; data voice, images, video on integrated line; fast call setup; secure, reliable, stable digital connectivity; efficient for bursty traffic

Comparing Connections, *con't.*

	Analog Dial-Up	Switched 56	Point-to-Point Leased Lines	Frame Relay	xDSL	Cable	ISDN	T-1, ATM/ Broadband ISDN
Weaknesses	• Slow • Old technology • Obsolete for modern data connections	Slow, by today's standards	Very expensive	Expensive (compared to ISDN), requires a dedicated access line, not widely deployed in capabilities Europe, expensive and complicated to make moves and changes	Standards and infra-structure still under development, service area distance limitations, degree of data transport symmetry varies	Voice on separate lin, connection shared with other users no firewall (security) capability	• High tariff rates • Complicated to install and configure	Not yet widely available; expensive, proprietary products can have mulitvendor compatibility problems

Low Speed - High Speed

CREATING A WEB SITE

Web sites are now common in corporate communications. Unfortunately, many developers don't understand the medium, so they're unsuccessful in communicating with their target audiences.

Another problem is thinking that web development is a one-person job; or, even worse, the boss has a nephew who can do the job really cheap. Big mistake.

Web site development requires skills in sales and marketing strategizing, copy writing, page layout, graphic design, and programming and electronic communications skills. These are just too many highly specialized skills for one person; even if you can find someone who's a Swiss army knife for web development, and the process may be quite lengthy.

There is a thirteen-step approach to site development that can help you get started.

72. How do I create a plan for my site?

Creating a web site is like building a house: You need a plan before you can start. Get everyone involved and brainstorm. Hold several sessions. Get as much information as possible. Don't hold back: brainstorming is supposed to generate new ideas, so don't let budgets, time, resources or other limitations hinder your thinking at this stage.

Do not plan as you go. The process will take longer, cost more, create unnecessary frustration, and in most cases will not get finished.

Make a top-ten list from the brainstorming session that represents the things you can do within your time period and budget. Be realistic. Ask consultants or web development companies for quotes and time lines.

Plan for the future as well as the present. Develop a phased approach over two years. (Given the advances in technology anything beyond two years will be obsolete by the time you're ready to implement it.) Whatever you plan to do, do it right or not at all.

73. How do I target my audience?

Identify your users. Are they corporate or home users? Corporate visitors will typically have faster Internet access, a good thing to know if you want to incorporate features that take a long time to download.

What kind of information or services will your visitors want from you? How much computer experience are they likely to have? New users need things simpler.

Be as specific as possible. Distinguish whether your visitors are purchasers or influence the purchasing decision. Assess their education level. Figure out what will keep your audience coming back to the site.

74. How do I identify the goals and objectives of my sites?

The goal for the site is what you would like to happen after your visitors have looked at your site. A sample goal might be that reviewing information about our company and looking at our product line, a customer will buy our product or make plans to buy it in the future.

The objectives must be measurable. This is how you benchmark the content of the site. Some sample objectives might be that:

- The site will provide visitors with our phone and fax numbers, address, and directions to our offices.

- The site will allow visitors to buy all our products online using Visa, MasterCard and American Express.

- The site will give visitors the total purchase cost, including shipping and taxes, before they enter their credit card number.

- Sales from the site will make up three percent of gross sales the first year, five percent the second year, and 10 percent the third year.

- The site will reduce phone calls to the receptionist requesting phone numbers, addresses, and other general information by five percent.

Objectives must not be too ambiguous. The following objectives are ambiguous:

- The web site will be hot and happening.

- Our site will be cooler than those of our competitors.

- We will use the site to increase sales.

The following are measurable objectives but they are not good reasons for having a web site:

- With online sales, we can eliminate our sales force (or other employees). *E-business will not eliminate the workforce; it should complement it, allowing your employees to be more productive and your company more profitable.*

- We can't put money into the web until we know it will be profitable. *This is bad bean-counter logic. As in the above explanation, e-business should turn out to eliminate redundant and low-level tasks and complaints about your business process.*

75. How do I determine the programming requirements for my site?

A lot of sites are done in Hyper Text Markup Language (HTML), so that is a given, but look at other things that you may need. Aspects to consider are the following:

- *JavaScript* is a script language with short programming commands that allow buttons to give a pressed appearance when you roll over them with a cursor. These commands can also detect a person's browser type, computer platform, and all kinds of other things.

- *Java* is a programming language used to create Java applets. These small programs, not scripts, are used to add date and time to the site, automate banners, create navigational aids, and many other actions.

- *Databases:* If you want to connect one to the web, you'll have to know how. There are lots of products that may make the process much easier. Do your research before you begin.

- *Flash:* Flash is an animation package that lets you use vector graphics on the web (otherwise you'll have to use bit-mapped graphics, which are lesser quality). Flash also provides smaller files for animation and interactivity.

- *Common Gateway Interface (CGI)* scripts automate the process for online forms.

- *E-Commerce:* Many e-commerce packages are available. Some are more extensive than others and prices range from a few hundred to hundreds of thousands of dollars. Figure our your needs and purchase a package that meet these needs and your budget.

Definitions:

Applet: A small application, that is typically used to provide one function—display time, automatically saves files, etc.

Common Gateway Interface (CGI): How HyperText Transfer Protocol Daemon-compatible (HTTPD-compatible) web servers should access external programs. If this process is followed, data will be returned to the user as a generated web page. CGI programs or scripts are commonly employed as a user fills out an on-screen form. The form generation or search process then brings other programs into play. After completing the on-screen form, you get a confirmation, feedback, another web page, etc.

HyperText Markup Language (HTML): A programming language used to develop a web site. One of the uses of HTML is to mark the site and all the hyperlinks within it.

HyperText Transfer Protocol (HTTP): An Internet standard supporting Web exchanges. By creating the definitions for URLs and their retrieval throughout the Internet, HTTP gives Web authors the ability to embed hyperlinks and also allows for transparent access to an Internet site.

Macromedia: A company that markets, among other things, authoring tools for multimedia. Go to *http://www.macromedia.com.*

Vector graphic (also called object-oriented graphic): A graphic composed of distinct elements, for example, lines, circles, ellipses, and boxes, that can be edited separately. These graphics are stored as mathematical formulae for the vectors or directional lines that compose the image.

76. How do I create the contents for my site?

Now that you're going to build a site, what are you doing to put in it? Asking yourself these questions will give you a good idea of how much work is in store for you.

- If you already have a site, what's wrong with it? What's right? Can any of it be used in the update? What does your target audience think about the site? Does it serve their needs?

- Do you have readably available photos, graphics, copy, or a database that can be transferred to the web site? Or, does everything have to be created from scratch?

- What's the quickest way for visitors to get around your site? The farther your visitors have to dig for information, the less likely they'll be to find it. What guidelines will be established for the site in terms of copy, navigation, and layout?

- How will you get visitors to come to your site, or return once they have been there? If you're an e-commerce site, show all pricing first. Display shipping charges before you ask for the credit card number.

77. How do I maximize the potential of the copy of my site?

The copy is certainly one of the most important part of the site. A poorly written site will discredit even the most beautiful graphics, or the most dazzling programming work. So:

- Get to the point. Nobody wants to read a lot of redundant rambling, no matter what it's about. A good strategy is to use as few words as possible.

- Does the copy give enough information for users to make a purchasing decision? Remember that if someone is buying a product from your site, there is no one immediately available to grab and ask a question, nowadays, and even e-mail takes too long.

- Are your titles and headlines descriptive? Again, most people want to get to the right place the first time. Don't confuse them with a section titled "support" and another titled "service."

- Make sure your copy goes through an editor, even if you have to hire one. A good editor can make quite a difference in your copy.

78. How do I work with the graphics of my site?

A graphics person who's a whiz at the paper brochure is not necessarily an online graphics specialist. The web is a totally different medium. Just because you reign in the printed world, doesn't make you monarch in the digital realm.

- Make sure your artist understands phrases, knows how to implement optimized graphics and web-safe colors, and knows the differences between browsers (Internet Explorer, Netscape Navigator, and America OnLine).

- Take into consideration that you can create design elements, like colored tables and text, in HyperText Markup Language (HTML). Talk with your site programmer and work out the specifics.

TIP: Determine the screen size for the site. The pallet of your site is determined by the size of the monitor. Use the chart below to determine the layout of your site's pallet.

Monitor Description	Pallet Width	Pallet Height	Screen Resolution
14" (All)	600	300	640 x 480
17" Windows	760	420	800 x 600
17" Mac	795	470	832 x 624
19" (All)	955	600	1024 x 768
Web TV	544	378	640 x 480

TIP: Use the gif wizard site (*http://www.gifwizard*) to check your posted web page for bloated graphics and poorly written HTML coding.

Definitions:

Graphics Interchange Format (GIF): A bit-mapped graphics file format often used for graphics exchange on a Bulletin Board System (BBS) and networks; it uses a high-resolution graphics compression technique.

79. How do I maximize the usefulness of my site?

- Provide opportunities for user feedback. One of the most common features of a web site is providing a user feedback on clickable areas. These features are usually triggered when a user rolls over a hotspot. The hotspot can be a button or link, and will create a visual effect, changing color, looking like a button that's depressed, or providing additional information about the topic rolled over.

- Use database integration. If you add a database to your site (such as product or services) be sure to make use to give the user some control over how the information is presented. For example if users want to search for the widgets, provide an option for them to see only the widgets in a specific price range, or sort the list from lowest to highest price.

- Use crawling or scrolling text. Text crawls (text that moves horizontally across the screen, like weather alerts on television), or scrolls (same thing except moves vertically on the screen) are often used to display stock prices, company news, or breaking events. Information contained within a crawl is often dynamic, or changing—or at least it seems that way.

- Use cookies to their full potential. A cookie is a small file that a web server puts on a visitor's hard drive. This file stores information about where the user has been on your site, and gives you an idea of the most popular sections of the site. Cookies can also be used to store user's personal information, such as name, address and buying preferences. This information can expedite on-line ordering because it accesses information that you have already entered.

TIP: Newer browsers (Netscape 6 and Internet Explorer 5) provide built-in feedback that requires no additional programming.

CAUTION: Cookies can also used to steal personal information. If you employ them, post an explanation of how they'll be used on your site. Reassure visitors that you'll never sell their personal information and that you're using cookies only to enhance the user experience.

80. So, how do I put all these steps together?

First, plan how you'll create the web pages: Will you use HTML by hand or use a program like as GoLive, Dreamweaver, Flash, or FrontPage?

Create the site from scratch: You can use a text editor (Wordpad or Simpletext) or a word processor (Word or WordPerfect). But be careful because Word creates some really messy HTML code. In other words, it may not look right in your browser and you'll spend a lot of time cleaning it up to make it look right. Some programs, like Dreamweaver, will clean it up for you. But they can't be counted on totally.

You can also use Netscape Communicator's Composer function, which will create adequate HTML code.

Decide which version of HTML you'll use. The big sites write to the latest standard to take advantage of its new features. Besides, browsers are now free, so most people upgrade to the latest version as soon as they come out.

TIP: Check out the World Wide Web Consortium (*http://www.w3.org*) for news on the latest version of HTML and more advice on web standards and design.

NOTE: If you want your site to look great in Microsoft Internet Explorer but not Netscape Navigator/Communicator, use FrontPage. It creates code that works very well with Microsoft products but not as well with their competitors.

If you choose to create the site from a text editor, we recommend *HTML 4 for the World Wide Web* (4th ed.: Peachpit Press, 1999) by Elizabeth Castro—a great book for starting out and as a reference.

Definitions:

Dreamweaver (Macromedia): A tool for site managers and for people who manage lots of pages or update content regularly. See *http://www.macromedia.com.*

Flash (Macromedia): A tool for making high-end sites with lots of inter-activity, it's an artist's tool but does require knowledge of HTML. See *http://www.macromedia.com.*

FrontPage (Microsoft): A low-end program for writing pages for use in the Web.

GoLive (Adobe): A tool for web designers and graphic and artistic peo-ple. See *http://www.adobe.com.*

81. Posting your site on the web

When you're ready to post your site on the web, you'll need a place to put it. This is called site hosting; it refers to a server who is "hosting" your site for display on the Internet.

There are two options for hosting the site. One is to set up the Internet server yourself, which requires that you have a server that is always con-nected to the Internet, a firewall to shield it from hackers, and the knowl-edge to administer the server. This option can be expensive. The second is to hire an ISP. The second option requires a monthly fee.

You'll also need a domain name. This is basically your address, what comes before the dot and the extension. You can set up a domain name at *http://www.networksolutions.com.*

When you have a place to put your site, you'll need to upload it to the server. This requires a file transfer program (FTP), which enables you to send files over the Internet.

TIP: Programs such as Dreamweaver, GoLive, and FrontPage have built-in FTP capabilities; check your manual on how to use them. Windows includes a standard FTP program with Windows 95 and newer versions. If you're using a Mac, you can use Dartmouth's FTP program, Fetch (located at: *http://www.dartmouth.edu/pages/softdev/fetch.html.*

NOTE: Don't forget site tracking: In most cases you'll want to track the usage of your site. You can do this with cookies, by the server, or by adding JavaScript to each page. There are many other options as well, so discuss your needs with your technical people.

Definition:

Domain name: On the Internet, a system of easily identifying individual servers or sites by using a single word or abbreviation. The domain name farthest to the right of an Internet address is the most general or top-level domain.

82. How do I market and advertise my site?

- Include your web site address on all your stationary. Since a web site is part of your corporate communications program, it should be considered another address for your organization.

- Issue a press release to announce your new site, or site redesign. Link to other sites, such as organizations in which you're a member or companies you do business with.

- Register the site with a search engine. There are many places to go to submit your site; some charge a fee, while others offer the same service for free. One of the free ones is Jim Tools at *http://www.jim-tools.com.*

- Use <Meta> tags in your site to help search engines find your pages. Some examples are: <META name="keywords" content= "widget, USA, manufacturing, reseller, service"> or <META name="description" content="Acme Toy company makes all kinds of cool toys for girls, and boys.">

Definitions:

<META> tag: A tag used in HTML to aid in identifying some of the elements in a web page. These tags can hold descriptions, search engine keywords, and more.

Search engines: Servers that run software, also called software robots (bots) or spiders. These engines search the Web for sites/pages that match your query.

83. Which search engines use descriptions or <META> tags?

Every search engine uses a different system to display your pages. Trying to get your organization at the top of every page will net about as much success as trying to locate the pot of gold at the end of a rainbow. Here are the major search engines and their tag usage:

- *AltaVista:* Uses <META> tags to index your site.

- *Excite:* Does not use <META> tags; instead, tags are automatically generated by Excite, which looks for common words or phrases within a page.

- *Hotbot:* Uses both keywords and description <META> tags.

- *Lycos:* Will automatically create a titles and description for your site from the text contained within your Web page.

- *WebCrawler:* Indexes by the text contained within the <TITLE> tag.

- *Yahoo!:* Requires you to go to the section that best describes your company (such as business > widgets > manufacturer) and then click on the "Suggest a Site" link at the very bottom of the page.

- *InfoSeek:* Uses both keywords and description <META> tags. The description contains up to 200 text characters and the keywords can include up to 1,000 text characters.

CAUTION: Don't repeat versions of a keyword more than seven times. If you do, InfoSeek will disregard your site.

TIP: Search engines can take some time to record your site. Here are some anticipated times for some of the major sites (as of early 2000):

- 1-2 weeks: AltaVista, Info Seek

- 2-4 weeks: Excite, HotBot, Lycos, Web Crawler

- 6-8 weeks: Yahoo!

84. Should I create my site in-house or use outside vendors?

If you have the resources (time, money, expertise) to do it in house, then do it. If not, hire a consultant. Decide which skills you need from consultants, then interview them.

A couple of questions to ask yourself about a consultant are:

- Can I bet my job on this company?

- Is the consultant easy to do business with?

Some other suggestions to think about:

- Never sign a consultant's standard contract. Review it and revise it to fit your needs.

- Ask to see the consultant's business plan. Have the consultant provide written provisions in case he changes his direction.

Chapter 3
Utilities

UTILITIES

1.   How can I protect my system from viruses?

You must first acquire some special software for the job. (Once upon a time, Windows came with antivirus software, but no more). Most folks use McAfee or Norton Antivirus. Both are excellent full-featured programs for under 50 dollars.

For your home machine, you might be able to find some cheaper, less robust alternatives. I opt for the freeware InoculateIT Personal Edition by Computer Associates International. My company uses McAfee. Both are good safeguards against common threats. But nothing will substitute for consistent backups of all your important data.

If you have an Internet connection, go to one of our favorite sites, cws.internet.com/32menu.html and browse the list of useful 32-bit programs. Under "Utilities (non-winsock)," you'll find Virus Scanners. Clicking this will take you to a list of virus protection programs with reviews by the staff and other users as well as pricing and download information. Then you can do the following:

1. Install your scanner of choice and follow the instructions.

2. Go with the default settings at first (our recommendation) until you notice a problem or want to tweak some things.

3. If you have Microsoft Office products, make sure you enable "macro protection" if given a choice. Microsoft Word and Excel macros are prime targets for virus engineers, who create major havoc with special viruses designed to exploit macros.

4. Your new software will scan your system and probably allow you to create an emergency rescue floppy disk. Do it and keep it in a safe place with your Windows emergency disk (you did make one of those, right?).

TIP: McAfee has a component called Screenscan that scans files on your hard drive while a screen saver is running. You might notice that reviving the system from screen saver control becomes sluggish under Screenscan. I recommend disabling Screenscan or features like it in other antivirus programs. Better to schedule regular scans with a scheduling utility or simply remember to run a scan yourself from time to time.

NOTE: Most important, keep up with your software's virus information updates. New viruses are appearing all the time. You'll need to either allow your software to go online and retrieve an update or use your web browser to visit your software maker's home page and pick up your own update.

Definitions:

Macro: In Microsoft Office software, a special program letting the user customize or automate common tasks. Macros are vulnerable to viruses because they can create or delete files without user verification.

Transmission Control Protocol/Internet Protocol (TCP/IP): A very common method of sending information over a computer network linking many dissimilar computers. TCP/IP insures the accuracy of the information transmitted and received by breaking down the information into small packets and checking that all characters in each packet arrive in the same form that they were sent.

Winsock: Short for Windows Sockets, which is a Microsoft Windows programming interface between applications and the TCP/IP network connection. Winsock compliant applications are those that obey rules set by Windows Sockets for sending and receiving information via TCP/IP.

2. I suspect my hard disk drive might be damaged or contain errors. What can I do?

The easiest and most obvious tools for disk maintenance come with Windows. If you have trouble opening or deleting a certain file or installing a new program, check your hard disk drives:

1. Click on the Start button, Programs, Accessories, and then System Tools.

2. Click on ScanDisk.

3. Click on your hard drive from the list of available drives to check for errors in the top text box.

4. Click on the Standard button. This will verify that the size and location of all of your files and folders are as they should be.

5. Check the Automatically fix errors checkbox if you would rather not be present during the scan. This will allow ScanDisk to address problems without stopping for confirmation.

6. Click on Start.

7. If the Standard check doesn't fix the problem, run ScanDisk again and click on the Thorough button. The Thorough check will take much longer, as it goes over every portion of a hard disk to see if there are any physical errors. ScanDisk can't actually fix the damage but can mark the location and try to salvage most of what is occupying the damaged area.

8. Click on the Options button to the right to check basic scanning settings.

9. Click on the System and Data Areas button

10. Click on OK.

11. Click on the Advanced button in the bottom right to select options for logging the scan information or to change how ScanDisk handles errors.

TIP: Take a minute to disable any running programs (Word, Excel, screen savers, etc.) that might interfere with your scanning operation. Any programs that regularly write to your hard drive will affect ScanDisk, causing it to start the scan over again. Some running programs will show up as tiny icons in your System Tray (the area to the right of your task bar, next to the clock). Many of these running programs are not really essential. Double click these icons to see if they can be closed or disabled.

NOTE: Since Windows runs ScanDisk after every system crash or improper shutdown (which is probably pretty often), you may not need to run ScanDisk routinely. A Standard check once a month should catch any potential problems and either fix them or prompt you for further action.

3.   I want to make some of my big files smaller. How do I do this?

You need a compression utility. The de facto standard for PC file compression is WinZip by Nico Mak Computing, Inc. WinZip is available as shareware from numerous places on the Internet (my favorite is http://cws.internet.com/32menu.html. Look under Compression Utilities. Download the file and run it from your hard drive. Follow the installation instructions.) To use WinZip:

1. Open the WinZip program.

2. Click on File from the drop-down menu.

3. Click on New.

4. Select a location and name for your new file. Remember this location and name.

5. Select the files you would like to copy into your .zip file. Your original files will remain intact unless you change the value in the Action box. You can choose to move the files instead of copying them.

TIP: Normal Compression is great for 99.9 percent of the files you'll need to compress. If you would like to compress and later recreate an entire folder tree, then under Folders check Include Subfolders and Save extra folder info.

CAUTION: Do not use DriveSpace (offered by Windows). This utility can interfere with other software and could result in lost data.

NOTE: Other free zip utilities are available on the Internet but I only recommend WinZip. I have had problems with utilities claiming to be compatible with WinZip zip files. Since you'll probably be e-mailing compressed files to others, compatibility is very important. Currently, the shareware version of WinZip runs indefinitely and costs $29 to register (price as of publication).

Compressed copies of your selected files now exist within the new zip file. You can easily attach this smaller file to an e-mail or copy it onto a portable medium for transport. E-mailers dislike receiving several unzipped files attached to a single e-mail or unnecessarily large files. In addition, most e-mail users will be familiar with zipping to compress and decompress files.

Other file compression formats exist but .zip files are most common on the Internet. WinZip also works great for a number of other formats.

TIP: Using file compression to archive old files and compress files for e-mail is a great idea. However, I don't recommend utilities that claim to compress your entire hard drive. This can lead to a wide variety of problems. Since current hard drive prices are low, it would be worth your money to invest in more hard drive and avoid messing with your system.

4. I've received a zipped file. What do I do?

We must assume you have WinZip or a similar utility program. When you receive a zip file:

1. Open WinZip.

2. Find the file (usually a Find command in the drop-down menu).

3. Double-click on the file.

4. Click on Extract to decompress some or all of the files to a location you select.

TIP: You can also simply drag and drop files to and from the WinZip window to add or extract. Make note of the folder where you place your extracted files, as things can easily be misplaced.

Definitions:

Shareware: A method of selling software that allows the user to copy and distribute software without permission. Users are asked to pay a modest fee to the software authors and to promise not to alter the software in any way. Sometimes shareware will continuously prompt you for payment before starting (nagware) or will stop working after several days of use without payment (crippleware).

Zip file: A compressed file created using PKZip or WinZip, which will have a .zip extension after the name. By opening the file, the user can add or extract files of other types to or from the compressed zip file.

5.   I need to find out more about my computer system. How do I do this?

Whenever you ask for help with a computer problem, the person you ask always wants to know as much about your machine as possible. Windows comes with a utility to show you the answers to most basic configuration questions. If you have Windows 98:

1. Click on Start, Programs, Accessories, System Tools, and then System Information.

2. All the information this person needs will probably be here, such as:

• Processor make (but not model)

• Installed RAM

• Installed hard disk drives

- Current Windows and Internet Explorer version (including the extended version number, which identifies exactly which patched version, after the initial release, is currently installed).

- Hardware resources: Shows information useful if you have a problem with conflicting cards or other peripherals. Conflicts/Sharing and IRQs provide answers to the simplest of these issues.

- Components: not much use to the end user—leave this one to the technicians.

- Software environment: Provides two interesting options: (1) Startup Programs gives a true list of programs that will automatically run at Windows startup. Quite a few of these don't appear in the Startup folder under your Start Bar. (2) Running Tasks gives a complete list of programs running at the moment. This is especially handy for policing programs that didn't shut themselves down properly.

All of this information can be easily read and saved for printing or e-mailing to a technician. To save this information:

1. Click on the File drop-down menu.

2. Click on Save.

3. Choose a name and location. If you'd like to e-mail your information, save it as a .txt file by selecting All Files (*.*) in the Save As box and typing your filename with a .txt extension. This will save all of the information in a simple text file for easy reading by anybody.

If you have Windows 95:

1. Click on the Start button, Settings, Control Panel, and the System icon.

2. Click on the Device Manager tab. This tab displays all of your installed hardware and software devices. If you click on a group of devices, the tree will expand to show all of the installed items

in that group. If any of the icons have a small exclamation point or X on the icon, there is some problem with that device. If an Interrupt ReQuest (IRQ) conflict exists, Windows may disable one of the conflicting devices and flag it with an exclamation mark.

3. Click on the General tab to display basic Windows information like your complete Windows version number, your registration name and ID, your processor make, and installed RAM.

4. Click on the Performance tab to access settings for your File System, Graphics, or Virtual Memory. These settings should not be altered except by a technician.

You can see a list of programs running currently at any time by pressing Ctrl+Alt+Delete. This brings up the Close Program box with a list of running programs and buttons, allowing you to shut down programs you select. DO NOT press Ctrl+Alt+Delete a second time unless you want to reboot your system.

Definitions:

Interrupt ReQuest (IRQ): Numbered IRQs are used by system devices to identify themselves and their needs to the central processing unit. Generally, devices can't share IRQ numbers. If two devices are trying to use the same IRQ, one or both may not function properly. This method of organizing peripheral computer devices is growing obsolete as alternative technologies like Universal Serial Bus and Firewire become more popular.

Random Access Memory (RAM): A special type of memory managed by operating system software. Unlike the hard disk drive, RAM stores information in active electronic circuit patterns, allowing much faster access to information; however, the information is lost when the power is turned off.

6.   I want to know about a system crash before it happens.

Most system crashes or lockups are the result of conflicting software. This will likely start as soon as you make some change to your system and only stop when you either undo the change or fix the problem.

Insufficient free hard drive space can sometimes cause system instability. Windows will probably warn you automatically if it requires more hard disk room. But with most modern hard drives, unless you're a serious multimedia user, you probably have acres of free space. For instance, you shoud have three gigabytes for users running current word processing or spreadsheet applications.

But often crashes result from a lack of free Random Access Memory (RAM). RAM is the fast access memory that Windows uses to run programs and itself. Often, programs stake out a portion of that memory for their exclusive use. Sometimes, those programs don't surrender all that memory when you shut them down. If you open and close a lot of applications in a short time, you might build up junk in your RAM—not a problem, until you do something that requires a large continuous piece of memory. Then, whammo. If the program can't deal with this and Windows can't deal with the program you're using, the system crashes.

Until software developers start making their programs behave better, you'll just have to keep an eye on available memory. To get information relating to your system and system crashes:

1. Click on Start, Programs, Accessories, System Tools, and then Resource Meter.

2. Up will pop a message notifying you that Resource Meter uses a small amount of your available memory itself. Click OK. A green bar-type icon will appear in your System Tray (that area in the lower right corner of your desktop).

3. Double-click on it, and it will give you a summary of available memory.

4. Below a certain amount of each type of memory, the meter drops into the yellow range. Save your work and check to see if you have an extra session of a program running or if you have a lot of files open at once. Close whatever you can and you might get back into the green. Eventually, you may have to restart your machine, so plan a coffee break.

5. If the meter shows red, save everything and restart immediately.

TIP: Copy the Resource Meter shortcut from System Tools to the Startup Programs portion of your start menu. This will load the Resource Meter each time you start your system.

Definitions:

System Tray: The area on the right side of the Windows Start Bar. Usually next to the clock, the System Tray contains a few small icons representing running programs. Double-clicking each one will usually open the program or give you more information.

7. Is there an easier way to view the images on my hard drive?

Images are tough things to keep organized because their filenames are often not descriptive enough to tell you what they look like. You might be able to set up Windows to generate thumbnails for images, but the results can be excruciatingly slow, especially if your machine already has a hard time with other imaging applications.

Unfortunately, Windows doesn't come with any good image management tools. Fortunately, many shareware or freeware options are available. Check out cws.internet.com/32menu.html for a current list and good reviews. My favorite graphics shareware utility is ACDSee, which at this writing costs $49.95 to register. Until you pay, ACDSee will nag you with random reminders while the program is running.

To download ACDSee:

1. Go to *http://cws.internet.com/32menu.html.*

2. Scroll down to Multimedia and Graphics in the right-hand column.

3. Click on Graphics/Images Tools.

4. Scroll down to ACDSee and click on it to download.

5. Download the installation file, following the instructions to install. Pay special attention to the portion of the installation that affects file associations. Unless you're a power graphics person,

you'll probably want to stick with the default—but if you do, graphics files will trigger this program when they're opened. ACDSee does provide access to other image viewers or editors via its Shell option.

The biggest advantage of ACDSee is its speed. It can decode image files so quickly that it doesn't have to resort to saving and constantly updating clumsy caches of temporary thumbnail images. It can read and display thumbnails amazingly fast, even on a slower machine. But it's strictly for image management; it doesn't have image manipulation tools. On the plus side:

- You can switch from viewing a whole directory of thumbnails to a full-size version of an image with a simple Return. Another Return takes you back to thumbnail view again.

- Zooming is as simple as pressing the + or the : button (no more looking for those tiny magnifying glass icons).

- Use the options under the View drop-down menu to control the look of your image browser screen layout.

- Click on Thumbnails under the Options drop-down menu to control the size of your thumbnails.

- When switching to single-image view, you can set the program to shrink the image to fit your available screen when necessary; this eliminates the annoying need to pan and zoom on an image when you just want to take a look at it. Go to Options, Viewer tab for this feature.

Definitions:

Home page: A web page used by an individual or organization to provide visitors with an introduction and basic information. Links to other pages with more specific information may be provided on the home page.

Thumbnail: A tiny version of a larger, more detailed image.

8. How can I keep my files secret or protected from others?

Windows allows you to set certain "attributes" on files. Select a file, then go to File, Properties and check the boxes for Hidden or Read Only. As the names imply, these will hide and protect files from changes. You can do the same with folders.

The problem with these safeguards is that they defend only against accidents. Anyone can easily view "hidden" files or change their "read-only" status.

Third-party software provides much better safeguards. I found iProtect, an Irish invention, on the *PC Magazine* web site. Its list of award winners often provides cheap reliable utilities.

1. Go to *http://www.zdnet.com/pcmag/*.

2. Type iProtect in the Search text box.

3. Click on GO.

4. Scroll down to the Downloads category.

5. Click on iProtectv1.3

6. Download and install it by unzipping to a temporary directory and run the .exe file. Follow the instructions to install.

7. You'll need a password. Don't forget it! As always, select one with at least eight characters including a couple of numbers. You'll be unable to start the program again without the password. Period. Ever. This is the most vulnerable part of the program so choose a serious password. Don't use anything as obvious as your name, names of friends or family, birth dates, or Social Security number.

The nice thing about iProtect is the interface. It looks a lot like Windows Explorer with some extra buttons. Simply select files or folders and click on one of the following buttons:

- *Lock:* Prevents changes and also viewing of the contents of a file or folder.

- *Hide:* Prevents the file or folder from showing up in programs or Windows Explorer at all, even when your Folder Options are set to Show All Files.

- *Encrypt:* Uses a truly hearty encryption algorithm called Blowfish with a 440-bit key. It takes a second to encrypt or decrypt, but this is serious stuff.

At the time of this writing, a user license for iProtect cost $79.95.

Definitions:

Attributes: Four special tags on Windows files. You can see which attributes are set on a file by right-clicking on it and selecting Properties. At the bottom of the display you should see check boxes next to Read-Only, Hidden, Archive, and System. When checked, Read-Only prevents changes to a file. Hidden keeps files from showing up in Windows Explorer (unless you select View, Folder Options, View tab, and check Show All Files). Archive tells Windows programs which files should be backed up. System identifies files critical to Windows that cannot be deleted or altered and do not appear in Windows Explorer (unless you select View, Folder Options, View tab, and check Show All Files).

Encryption algorithm: To encrypt data, a program must transform that data to make it unreadable. Since the data must be decrypted later, the encryption process must be reversible. Encryption programs use a complex mathematical process (an algorithm) to generate the transformed file. The process is based on a long string of characters called a key. The longer and more random the key, the harder it is to reverse the transformation and decrypt the file.

9. How can I get rid of computer files I no longer need?

Windows 98 comes with disk management tools to help you manage your huge collection of files.

To get rid of unwanted files, do the following:

1. Click on the Start button, Programs, Accessories, System Tools, and then Disk Cleanup.

2. Click on the disk you want to clean.

3. Instruct Disk Cleanup to scan the disk.

4. Disk Cleanup will present you with a list of options and the amount of space deleting each group of files will restore. Select those options you desire.

5. You'll save the most space by deleting Temporary Internet Files and Temporary Files. Windows gives you a description of each category when you select it and may give you the opportunity to review a list of the files to be removed.

6. Use the More Options tab to give access to two standard Control Panel tools: Windows Setup and Add/Remove Programs for removing applications you no longer find useful.

The Settings tab lets you trigger Disk Cleanup whenever Windows runs low on disk space.

NOTE: If you're a Windows 95 user, or if you want more rigorous policing of old files that programs leave behind, try a third-party utility like HDValet from *PC Magazine*. This is a free utility that scans for common backup files, log files, and temporary files that programs can orphan.

To download HDValet:

1. Go to *http://www.zdnet.com/pcmag/*.

2. Type HDValet in the Search text box.

3. Click on GO.

4. Scroll down to the Downloads category.

5. Click on *PC Magazine's* HDValetv1.1.

6. Download the compressed file to your system.

7. Extract the files, using WinZip or a similar file compression/decompression program, to a temporary directory on your hard drive and run the file called install.exe. Remember where you saved the file.

TIP: You must have file compression software that will handle zip files already installed on your computer. See question 3 for information on where to locate WinZip and how to handle compressed zip files.

Note that:

- When you run HDValet, you'll see a list of default types of "junk" files. Each type has a default Cleanup action associated with it.

- To see what HDValet will do when it encounters one of these files, select the file type and hit Ctrl+Enter. You'll see that most files will be sent to your Recycle Bin. If you discover that you need a removed file later, you should be able to restore it from the Recycle Bin (if you haven't emptied it since then).

- You can add new "junk" file types to HDValet. For instance, my CAD software creates troublesome little configuration files for each file I create. I can setup HDValet to scan for these files by their extension and move them to the Recycle Bin, where I can restore or delete them at my leisure.

If you operate the program with the Test Mode box checked, HDValet will take no action but will generate a list of each file and its associated action. You can use Test Mode to make sure that nothing vital gets moved.

If you want to clean up old documents, the best way is to use the tools that come with Windows Explorer:

1. Open Windows Explorer

2. Press Ctrl+f (or click on Tools, Find, and then Files or Folders). This opens the Find Files utility.

extension and location.

4. Use the Date Modified tab to look for files by when they were created or last accessed. This will help you avoid moving files created long ago but viewed every day.

5. Use the Advanced tab to find files by size or containing precise text.

6. When Find Files is finished scanning, it will display a list of results. You can Move, Copy, or Delete any or all of the files listed just as you would in the main Explorer window.

TIP: While it might seem like a good idea to let a program periodically look for older documents or system files, nothing substitutes for careful daily file management. In my experience, automatic utilities lead to mysteriously lost files and confusion because users forget the utilities are operating. I like to take a few minutes about once a month to use all the techniques listed above. This way nothing happens without my knowledge and nothing will surprise other company or home users if they must access my system while I'm away from my computer.

Definitions:

Computer Aided Design (CAD) or Computer Aided Drafting and Design (CADD): Software used to generate extremely precise drawings or models for engineering production, building construction, product testing, or special effects. See "I Want to Draw an Object in Three Dimensions" in the Graphics section below for more information on CAD software.

Log file: A simple text file that keeps careful notes of the actions of a program. It can be very helpful if you're troubleshooting a problem. These files can have a variety of extensions and may be created and deleted automatically. Check the program's diagnostic tools for logging options.

Chapter 4
Graphics

GRAPHICS

The key to understanding most graphics files and programs is the concept of resolution.

Most graphics files you might use are composed of individual dots of color called *pixels*. Sharper images require more pixels. More pixels means that the file contains more data and takes up more disk space. Image quality is a careful balance between the amount of data in an image file and the level of quality you desire.

If you wish to change the size at which an image is displayed without reducing image quality, you must change the *resolution* of the image. Resolution is usually expressed in pixels per inch (ppi). Displaying or printing an image at a resolution of 150 ppi produces a sharper image than displaying or printing at 75 ppi. Changing the resolution doesn't change the quality of the image. Resolution just determines the image size.

But note that a difference exists between file size and image size. Because graphics files contain a lot of information, they can be hard to send over networks or store on smaller media like floppies. By compressing an image, you can reduce the file size. Certain types of image files are compressed and some are not. This section explains which file formats are right for your needs.

When working with images, avoid *resampling*. Resampling an image actually changes the number of pixels and will adversely affect image quality.

NOTE: There are a huge number of graphics software packages. Here we give basic instructions to give you a general idea of the steps for an average package. The exact steps, however, may be different.

IMAGE ISSUES

1.   I want to get a picture into my computer. How do I do this?

Do you already have a photographic print you'd like to use? You'll need access to a scanner. Scanners are fairly inexpensive nowadays. I recommend Hewlett-Packard scanners, primarily for their proven compatibility with a variety of systems and software. Look for a flatbed model (at least legal size) with backlighting capabilities, which will allow you to scan transparencies and even 35mm slides. To get the picture:

1. Decide how big you want the image to be in your final document or display.

2. Scan the image at a resolution that provides about 150 pixels per inch. This should display well on screen and in most office documents, though it may not be adequate for professional "magazine" quality printing; for these requirements, contact the publisher.

See question 9 for tips on formatting your image.

You don't have a photo but you found an image on the web? Beware of copyright violation. Ask permission before using any image from the Internet. See question 14 for more detail.

Need to take the photo from scratch?

- A digital camera is the way to go. Prices are affordable, perhaps even low enough to merit buying instead of renting. For anything besides professional publishing, a camera capable of 1024x768 24-bit color images will suffice.

- The camera should be able to download images directly to your computer via cable and perhaps also via other media like floppy disk or Personal Computer Memory Card International Association (PCMCIA) compatible media. This is the fastest way of obtaining an original image for everyday digital use.

Definitions:

Personal Computer Memory Card International Association (PCMCIA): A special style of expansion port designed primarily for laptops and sometimes used in small devices like digital cameras.

24-bit: A measure of color depth in a graphic image. Bits refer to the actual amount of information needed to represent the color of an individual pixel. 24-bit images require 24 bits of information to define an individual pixel. This yields up to 16,777,216 possible colors.

2. The image I scanned looks really blocky and grainy. Why is that?

You might be limiting Windows to too few colors. Try changing your Windows display properties:

1. Click on Start, Settings, Control Panel, and then the Display icon.

2. Click on the Settings tab.

3. Check that the Colors text box reads a minimum of 256.

4. Check that the Screen Area has at least 800 x 600 pixels (again, the bigger the better).

Windows will test the new settings if necessary and ask you to approve them. When you set the colors Windows can use, you limit it to those colors. Any color that doesn't lie within that set must be simulated by screen *dithering*. Dithering is less noticeable in some programs because they may be designed to use 256 or fewer colors.

No luck? Try another scan:

1. Rescan the image and make sure you don't scan it at too low a resolution.

2. Use settings appropriate for a laser printer, about 150 pixels per inch (ppi).

3. Make sure to save the image in a format that supports the full color range. Try .bmp or .tif format if you'll be doing a lot of editing on the image. If you need to keep the image small and don't intend to work on it, use the .jpg format.

Still no luck? Does the image look bad to begin with? Don't expect scanning to correct basic flaws, especially poor focus. Good photo editing software can be used to erase scratches, rebalance colors, and change brightness and contrast, but too much alteration can be more difficult than simply retaking a photo.

Definitions:

Bitmap graphic: Any graphic file format that defines each pixel individually. Generally, bitmap graphics are not compressed, so they can be extremely large. This is the opposite of a vector graphic (see below).

.bmp (file): An uncompressed bitmap-type graphic file. You can save .bmp files in a Windows-compatible form or an OS/2 (IBM) compatible form. Because they're not compressed, they can be quite large, but like most uncompressed files, they maintain the quality of the original scan by representing pixels individually.

Dithering: The process of reassigning scan colors not included in your software's color palette to the nearest match within the available palette. Dithering methods use mathematical algorithms to decide which colors to substitute for which. Whenever possible, dithering should be avoided because it requires additional processing time and produces images that are not faithful to the original. Set your Windows display to show as many colors as possible (see question 3).

.jpg or .jpeg: A compressed bitmap-format graphic file that compresses images by looking for large areas of single or similar color pixels and representing them as a group rather than as individual pixels. This method works well for photographs but tends to unnecessarily soften line art. There are .jpgs all over the Internet because they're quite small and therefore transmit quickly. JPEG stands for Joint Photographic Experts Group.

Pixel: A single dot of color in a graphic image. Graphics files contain the data necessary for software or hardware to reproduce images. The most basic unit in an image is the pixel. When many very tiny pixels are viewed together, the result is a coherent image. Computer monitors compose pixels from small trios of red, green, and blue dots. Each pixel on your screen is some combination of these colors (except for black, which is represented by no color). The resolution is expressed in the number of pixels per displayed inch (ppi) or the image dimensions measured in pixels (horizontally x vertically).

Vector graphic: Any graphic file format that defines an image geometrically. Lines are mathematically represented as two points in 2D or 3D coordinates. Circles are represented as a single center point and a radius. Fills or subtle color changes can also be represented as a mathematical process. Thus, vector graphics contain instructions on how a program should draw the image. Often vector graphics are smaller than bitmap graphics because less information is required to reproduce the image. They are also truly scalable: they can be reduced or enlarged without affecting image quality. Lines remain sharp at all times.

3. The image I scanned looks great except for a really ugly object. How do I fix this?

Does the object interfere or overlap with the main subject? If so, crop it out:

1. Look for a crop tool (usually represented by overlapping right angles) or use the selection tool to create a rectangle around the good part.

2. Go up to the menu and select an option like "Crop" or "Crop to selection."

Is the main subject very simple with only a couple of shades? If so, paint out the object:

1. Find the Color Picker tool (usually looks like an eyedropper) to sample a color from the main subject. This should make the color you choose the current color used for painting.

2. Find the Paintbrush tool. Click and drag to paint over the offending object. You should be able to make the paintbrush smaller or larger.

Does the main subject have a complicated pattern, like woodgrain or brick? If so, clone it out:

1. Look for the Clone tool or a tool that will sample one area and copy it to another as you move your brush.

2. Select the area to be copied (this is often done by right-clicking or shift+left-clicking).

3. Begin painting over the offending object by clicking and dragging. So long as you're holding down your mouse button, you'll be moving both your brush and the area you're sampling. The result is something like Bugs Bunny using a can of plaid paint; you can copy an entire area stroke by stroke.

TIP: Make sure you have several levels of Undo enabled (check the program's Options menu) because it's easy to make mistakes. If you can't control how many times you can Undo, when you open the image, immediately save it under another name before beginning work.

4.   Some of the lines in the drawing I scanned look broken or missing. What do I do?

Try zooming in on the image:

1. Select the Zoom tool (usually looks like a magnifying glass).

2. Click and drag your selection window around the offending area.

3. If the lines reappear when you zoom in, the problem is not the file but the limits of your display. Monitors only display about 96 pixels x 96 pixels per inch of screen. Scanned line art might represent lines with strings of pixels only one or two pixels wide. If the image is at a higher resolution, your video processor will have to show the pixels it can and skip a few here and there to make the whole thing fit into the size you want on screen. The information is still in the image, but your display adapter must ignore some of it, which can result in whole lines playing hide and seek.

4. If the lines still look broken when you zoom in, try scanning the image as a grayscale or a full-color image. This will capture more color variations from the original drawing and hopefully fill in some of the blanks.

Does the image look dull with grayish background and darker (but not black) lines? If so, try adjusting the brightness and contrast.

1. Check your graphics software for Brightness and Contrast adjustments. By increasing the contrast, you can make the drawing stand out a little more.

Do you really need the image to look good on screen?

1. If all the information is there but just not displaying well, ask yourself whether you really need it to look good on screen. The image will probably print fine.

2. If screen presentation is what you need, you'll probably have to compromise a little. Zoom in on the absolute most critical portion of image until the lines display clearly. You might have to crop the image to show only the parts you need.

TIP: Try to find a vector version of the image. If the drawing is computer-generated (a CAD drawing for instance), you can probably get the original vector file. See if the creator can convert it to a more generic Windows format like .wmf. Once in vector form the image should look fantastic at any scale and you can even edit the lines and shapes in programs like CorelDRAW, Microsoft Publisher, and even PowerPoint.

Definitions:

CAD or CADD: Computer-Aided Design or Computer-Aided Drafting and Design. CAD software is used to generate extremely precise drawings or models for engineering production, building construction, product testing, or special effects. See question 7 for more information.

.wmf (file): The extension for a Windows Metafile. This is a vector file designed for use in Windows applications. Generally, Windows Metafiles are used for simple shapes and clip art that must be scaled and stretched. Some programs can convert other vector files into .wmf files.

5. Someone sent me a picture attached to an e-mail but I can't see the picture. What can I do?

Did you find the file attached to the e-mail?

1. Look in the body of the message for a lot of garbled text. If you find a lot of bizarre characters where the message should be, one (or both) of you may have set your e-mail program to handle attachments incorrectly.

2. Look under the mail program's Options or Preferences menu for a file attachment option.

3. Set it for MIME-compatible attachments. If you don't have a MIME option, it might be time to upgrade your mail software. Plenty of free programs are available; start by upgrading with your web browser. Most browsers come with mail programs.

Do you have the same program your friend used to create the file?

1. Save the attachment as a file on your hard drive. Select the attachment and right-click for options.

2. Start the program used to create the file

3. Use that program's Open dialog box to open the file you just saved. Sometimes Windows might not recognize a file type, but that doesn't mean that the program itself won't recognize it.

Do you have a program similar to the one used to create the file? Saving the attachment as a file on your hard drive. To do this:

1. Click once on the file's icon to select it.

2. Then right-click over the selected file and you'll get a list of new options.

3. Among them should be an option to save the attachment. Select it and select a location on your hard drive.

4. If the file was edited or created in, say, Adobe Photoshop, try to open it using, say, Corel PhotoPaint or JASC Paintshop Pro. Start the program and use the File, Open menu to open the file from your hard drive. Often similar programs handle the same file formats.

If you don't have a graphics program (other than Windows Paintbrush), check out the Net for a freeware/shareware file viewer that reads lots of types of files or a graphics editing program like Paintshop Pro.

If these procedures don't work, you'll have to resave your file in another, more common format. Graphics come in all kinds of formats, but only a few can really be considered universal.

- For bitmap images try .jpg (aka .jpeg) files. Because JPEGs are common on web sites, they're read by any browser.

- Although .bmp files are common, they may have limits in the number of colors they can represent or may not compress well.

- For line drawings, .gif files are great.

- For vector graphics, try .wmf (Windows Metafile); if prompted, try to save text as fonts, not curves.

- Vector graphics alternatives are .cmx (Corel graphics exchange—version 5 is common) or .dxf (Autodesk drawing exchange file) used by CAD programs and most illustration packages.

Definitions:

.cmx (file): An image file saved in a Corel proprietary format. This format saves image information (including vector-based shapes) for editing in Corel software.

.dxf (file): A format created by Autodesk that saves only precise information for use in CAD or illustration software.

.gif (file): A compressed file format designed for line art and bold graphics. Various versions are in use; some support transparent colors and simple animation. A lot of advertising and icons on the Internet are .gif files. GIF stands for Graphics Interface Format.

Line art: Artwork primarily composed of lines, as opposed to graphics, which contain subtle color gradations or soft edges.

Multipurpose Internet Mail Extension (MIME): A fairly recent method of encoding non-text information like images to be read along with mail messages.

6. My images look great on screen, but when I print them they look lousy. What can I do?

Do your prints look patchy or blocky? Try adjusting your printer driver's dithering settings. These settings control how the printer uses ink to simulate the colors on your screen. To adjust the settings:

1. Click on the File drop-down menu.

2. Click on Print and then Properties.

3. From there, you should be able to access dithering controls. Look for settings like Fine Dithering or a special Photographic print mode.

Do your prints look striped? Try cleaning your printer.

1. If it's a laser printer, see your manual for the proper procedure.

2. If it's an ink jet, try using the printer's self-cleaning features or gently clean the cartridge nozzles with alcohol and a lint-free cloth.

3. Also, make sure your dithering settings are set (see immediately above) and use a high-quality paper designed for your type of printer.

4. Consult our discussion on Printers in chapter one.

Do your prints look totally black?

1. Check your printer options for a setting that prints all colors as black.

2. Make sure you deselect it and switch to either a full-color setting or grayscale.

7. I want to draw a three-dimensional (3D). How do I start?

First, do you need an actual 3D model or just a shape that looks 3D on your document? For 3D-*looking* shapes, you can use tools like those in PowerPoint, adjusting lines and shapes to simulate depth, shadow, and reflection:

- Find the 3D button on the drawing toolbar and click it to access your options. Also, look through the clip art that comes with programs like Microsoft Word or check the Internet for free clip art that looks 3D. You might be able to find what you want and insert it into your document.

- For an accurate 3D model, you'll need special software.

- A lot of graphics suites come with plug-ins or special stand-alone programs for creating shapes with three dimensions. But beware: This is harder than it seems. You'll be drawing in 3D on a 2D screen, which really takes some getting used to. If you can make do by using tools like those in PowerPoint, things will be a lot easier.

TIP: If you're committed to creating an actual 3D model of an object, evaluate what you really need first. Do you have to simulate special materials (like stone or water)? Do you want to light your shape with complex lights? Do you require really accurate shapes? If so, go to a reputable software dealer who knows the products (preferably someone who works a lot with graphic artists or architects) and ask what software package might work best for you. An affordable program like MiniCAD might suit you; but you might need heavy-duty CAD or modeling software, which can run thousands of bucks. If you can't get what you need, look in the Yellow Pages or the Internet under computer services. Every day, more companies are providing 3D modeling and rendering services. Most charge a substantial hourly rate, but their expertise will provide results fairly quickly.

8.   I have an image file, but none of my software can read it. How do I fix this?

First, does the file name have an extension—anything after the period? The extension tells Windows which program to use when opening the file.Though all file names have extensions (usually three letters long), sometimes Windows can be set to hide them.

- In Windows Explorer, if you can't see extensions for any of your files, go to View, Folder Options, View and uncheck "hide extensions for known file types."

- If the extension is missing, Windows won't know which program to use. If you can guess at the extension, try renaming the file to include your extension and then open it again.

If that didn't help, can you guess which program to use?

- Try to start a similar program and then open the mystery file from there. Sometimes programs can open or convert unknown files automatically.

If you still have no luck, see if the author of the file can help.

9. My image is taking up too much space on my hard drive (or taking too long to display). How do I fix this?

When you insert the image into a document, do you always have to shrink it or crop it? If so, your image is likely too large for your needs. To adjust it:

1. Try cropping the image. This will allow you to show only the most important part without sacrificing image quality.

2. If you can't crop the image, you'll have to resample it. Make a copy for safekeeping and resample the image in a graphics program like Adobe Photoshop or Corel PhotoPaint.

3. To determine the proper size, physically measure the final version of the image on your printed document or on screen. Assume you'll need about 150 pixels per final inch of image.

4. Then select the image size adjustment and select Resample. Adjust the image size in pixels to suit your needs. For example, a 6x4 image will require 900x600 pixels at 150 pixels per inch (ppi).

TIP: Avoid resampling whenever possible because the procedure can decrease image quality. If you must resample, do not change the proportions of the original image. Also, reduce the number of pixels by multiples of one-half. This will allow the software to simply eliminate pixels, minimizing quality loss.

If the file is still too big, try a new format. Some image formats save graphics pixel by pixel. Others look at areas where pixels are all a similar color and fudge a little bit to save some space. The former are called "lossless" formats because they don't lose any information from the original image when they save. The latter are called "lossy" because they discard bits of information that will have no noticeable effect on the image. For most uses, lossy formats are acceptable, but if an image is to be published professionally or blown up to a large size, lossless formats are necessary.

To try a new format:

1. First, save the original image someplace safe.

2. Then save it as a .jpg (JPEG) image. JPEG images are lossy but very efficient at compressing data. You'll find them all over the Internet for just that reason. Some software will allow you to control just how much quality you sacrifice when saving a .jpg image.

3. Experiment a little until you find the right balance between size and quality for your needs.

10. I want to print out an image at poster size. How do I do this?

There's good news and bad news:

The good news is that you can format an image so that it can serve you better for printing in large-format presentations. When creating an image (with an illustration program, scanner, or camera), you can generally specify the resolution to use when you save the image.

The bad news is that the image you have might not work. You might have to scan the image again or take a new picture. Resolution means the number of pixels the computer breaks an image into to store it. The fewer the pixels, the less detail is saved. When you blow up a low-resolution image, each individual pixel becomes obvious as a single colored square. When you blow up a high-resolution image, you don't see the pixels because there are many more of them within the picture. So:

- Try to plan ahead for large-format images. You'll have to save the image at high resolution and that means a much larger file size. That means they might not load fast enough for practical on-screen viewing or they will not fit on your storage media.

- A good rule of thumb is 100 pixels per inch (that is 100 horizontally and 100 vertically, for a total of 10,000 pixels per square inch) of the final print. Hence, a 36x24-inch poster image would require at least 3,600 horizontal pixels by 2,400 vertical pixels.

TIP: Some programs (like Corel PhotoPaint) also offer options for sizing the image in measured units like inches or centimeters. Be careful. Simply enlarging the dimensions of a picture will not make it print more clearly at large scale. Similarly, shrinking an image may decrease not the file size but only the default resolution at which the program shows you the picture. To be sure you're working with the right number of pixels in a given image, pay attention only to the number of pixels (e.g., 600x800, 1,024x768).

The other way to create an image for large printing is to make a vector graphic. Vector graphics differ from scanned images or digital photos because they aren't stored as pixels, they're stored as shapes, defined with coordinates and equations. Vector images usually take up less disk space than bitmapped images, but not always. Especially complex images with a lot of curves and complex blends of color can be quite large.

The real advantage of vector graphics is scalability. Since the shapes are stored mathematically, their size can be easily multiplied or divided without changing the image. Sharp thin lines stay sharp at any size and smooth curves always look nice and round. This makes vector graphics ideal for things like logos that can appear on everything from business cards to blimps.

- The easiest vector format to use is probably the Windows Metafile (.wmf file). It lets you create vector graphics in a lot of presentation programs and office suites.

- Look for drawing tools like circles, squares, triangles, and lines. You should be able to stretch and color these shapes to your heart's content. Just make sure you save them as a vector file or you'll lose the shape information and be stuck with a jaggy bitmap.

- Pay attention to the resolution quantity. Resolution means the number of pixels the computer breaks an image into to store it. The fewer the pixels, the less detail is saved. Resolution is expressed in either pixels per inch (ppi) or horizontal pixels multiplied by vertical pixels (e.g. 640x480, 1,024x768)

BUSINESS PRESENTATIONS

11. I want to put an image into my document. How do I do this?

Almost all word processors, spreadsheets, and even databases will allow you to import a graphic image from a file. To place a picture into your document:

1. Click in the File drop-down menu for an Import or Place option.

2. Click on Import (or Place).

3. Once there, find the directory where your image resides.

4. If the directory doesn't show up, check the File Type box to be sure you're not limiting your view to the wrong type of file.

If the above procedure doesn't help:

1. Go to the Insert menu and look for "Image," "Picture," or "Object."

2. Try "linking" the image so that changes you make to the graphic are automatically shown in your document.

3. Once you've inserted an image, try manipulating the image by stretching, flipping, cropping, etc.

TIP: If you inserted a vector file (like a Metafile .wmf), you might even be able to change some of the colors from within your document without changing the original file. For instance, in PowerPoint, right-click on your image and look for Properties. Then, go through the tabs until you find the Recolor button. This will let you replace colors in the Metafile. This can be handy for making elements disappear in slides; just replace the offending color with one that matches the background.

12. I want to use graphics in a presentation for an audience. How do I do this?

If you want to print big presentation boards, see question 10.

Do you want to use an overhead projector?

- You'll need to print your presentation on a printer that can handle transparencies, or print them on paper and photocopy onto transparencies.

- You might also be able to buy or rent a flat screen projector that can double as an overhead. This lets you use standard transparencies and also project your presentation directly from computer.

Do you want to use 35mm slides?

- You can easily take presentation files like PowerPoint files to a full service photography or copy store; they can produce actual slides from them. Allow a couple of days for this service. Ask the store how best to deliver the file to them.

Do you want to project directly from a laptop computer? If so:

1. Rent or buy a video projector. New projectors are expensive, so unless you're ready to invest a few thousand dollars, contact your local camera shop or copy shop about rentals.

2. Plan your schedule carefully since rental fees are high. If you need to save money, investigate hourly rentals.

3. Projectors connect to a laptop via the serial port for an external monitor, so check your connections in advance.

4. TEST your presentation. Practice unpacking your equipment and connecting all your cables as well as running your show.

TIP: Some projectors might require that you adjust your Windows display settings for 800x600 pixels or 640x480 pixels and 256 colors. If at all possible, take your computer to the rental store and try your presentation with a technician. Don't leave until you're comfortable that you can set up the projector by yourself.

Definitions:

Serial port: One of many ports allowing attachment of devices to your computer via a cable. A serial port sends and receives information over the same wires in the cable. This means that while information travels one way, returning information must wait until the first transmission is complete. Serial ports usually connect devices (e.g., mice, keyboards, or external monitors) that don't require two-way transmission.

13. My presentation is boring. How can I animate objects to spruce it up?

Would you like to make your slides dissolve or fade into one another? In PowerPoint, you can set up transitions between slides:

1. Go to Slide Sorter View.

2. Select the slides you want to change.

3. Select a transition from the Slide Transition Effects list box.

4. In the Slide Transition dialog box, choose a method for triggering the slide advance (automatically or on mouse click). You can also set a sound file to play during the transition.

5. Click Apply to All for all slides in your show or Apply for the slides currently selected.

Would you like to make your text and graphics fade in/out or slide in/out? In PowerPoint, you can set default actions for your text and objects or you can set them one at a time:

1. Switch to Slide Sorter View.

2. Select the desired slides.

3. In the Text Preset Animation list box, choose an effect.

TIP: Stay away from Random Effects. They can distract an audience from your main points.

To set an action for a specific object:

1. Go to Slide view.

2. Select Custom Animation from the Slide Show menu.

3. In the Custom Animation dialog box, you'll see a list of objects that can be animated. Use the arrows to change their order.

4. Select an object and use the Effects tab and other tabs to adjust effects and timings for the selected items.

Would you like to create a cartoon that actually does something?

This will require animation or video editing software. You'll likely end up scanning a drawing or creating one with the software's drawing tools. Then you'll be able to make the object follow a path and perform certain actions at specified points and times. Try Adobe Premier for full-featured animation, or try top graphics suites like Corel that come with some less robust animation tools.

14. I saw a great image on the Internet and I want it.

Have you checked the copyright status of the image? Almost everything you see on the Internet, as in print, is copyrighted. Check with the author before using. If you have no problem with copyright, then:

1. Save the image right away (stuff changes fast on the Internet):

2. In your browser, right-click over the image.

3. Select Save Image. (You'll be prompted for a location.)

4. Worry about editing the image later in your photo editing software.

TIP: Sometimes small versions of an image are used as pointers to a full-size version. These smaller images (thumbnails) are often far too small for use in a document or presentation. Click on the image to see if it links you to a better one. Or, skip a step and Select Save Target instead of Save Image and your browser will download the linked image without even opening it in your browser window.

15. I want to make a video for use in my presentation. How do I do this?

Do you already have a video file you'd like to use? If you do:

1. Go to the Insert menu in your presentation program and select Movie or Object.

2. Your program will give you options on how to start the movie (automatically or with a click).

You don't have a file, but you do have a video on tape? You'll either need to invest in a little hardware, or get some help. A small video production company, camera shop, or video-to-film conversion company might be able to scan your tape to a file.

TIP: Remember that video requires a lot of disk space, so be prepared to accept your file via CD-ROM or another large-format media.

You have an idea but nothing else? The best thing would be a digital video camera. You can rent, buy, or hire a small video production company. You should be able to store the necessary length of video in the camera's memory and then download the video as a file to your computer.

TIP: Do a test video first, and try it on your computer. The size of the video image and the format you choose may affect playback speed and smoothness. You might consider storing and running the video directly from a fast CD-ROM drive rather than your hard drive. This will save disk space and keep your video safe from accidental deletion.

16. I want sound in my presentation. How do I do this?

Do you want theme music?

- The easiest thing to do is to play a CD with your computer's CD-ROM while the presentation is running. Adding specially synchronized music to your presentation as a digital file may be more trouble than it's worth. Playing the sound file is an extra task that the computer will have to juggle along with your presentation. If your presentation contains video clips or high-resolution images, the sound might skip or stall occasionally while your computer switches priorities between sound and visual data processing. If you must synchronize, I suggest checking the Internet for small, repeatable sound clips. You can set PowerPoint to play the clip over and over without interruption. If the clip is small enough, the entire file will remain in your computer's RAM for fast access throughout your presentation. Definitely experiment with your selection first.

Do you want music in just a couple of places? You can insert a small sound file just as you would an image or movie:

1. Go to the Insert menu.

2. Select Movies and Sound, Sound from File.

3. In the Insert Sound dialog box, select the sound file you want. You'll have the option of triggering the file to play when the slide appears or on a mouse click. (Check the Internet for small, free sound clips for presentation use.)

Do you want to record your own music or sound?

- Recording new digital music well takes good hardware and software. Recording something from a CD to a digital file might be possible with your sound card. Copyright issues may be a problem; check with the music publisher.

If you want to record using Window's Sound Recorder:

1. Click on the Start, Programs, Accessories, Multimedia, and then Sound Recorder.

2. Click on the record button.

3. You'll be able to record a clip of up to two minutes, depending on the quality you select.

If you want to play a CD, and it doesn't play automatically through your CD-ROM:

1. Insert a CD in your CD-ROM device.

2. Click on Start, Programs, Accessories, Multimedia, CD Player

3. Click on the play button. The Sound Recorder should pick up any sound source connected to your sound card.

If the sound is too quiet or too loud:

1. Click on the Start, Programs, Accessories, Multimedia, and then Volume Control.

2. Click and drag the sliders for control of the relative playback volume of different sound sources. You'll normally want the Wave source to playback lower than the CD source. (You might never need to control the volume of a Musical Instrument Digital Interface (MIDI) source or a Line In source.)

3. Click on the Options drop-down menu.

4. Click on Properties and uncheck the volume controls you don't need (in the Show the following volume controls text box).

Definitions:

Musical Instrument Digital Interface (MIDI): A standard format for encoding digital sounds used by all sorts of electronic instruments and programs to save and reproduce music. Unlike regular sound files, MIDI files store individual instrument voices, which can be edited.

DISPLAY ISSUES

17. Everything on my screen looks blocky or patchy. Images that should look smooth look striped. How do I fix this?

Your Windows display settings may be too limiting:

1. Click on the Start button, Settings, Control Panel, and then the Display icon.

2. Click on the Settings tab.

3. Check the Colors box.

It should read at least High Color (16-bit). If it shows 256 colors or 16 colors, you are limiting Windows to a rather tiny palette. The various graphics and icons that must be displayed might contain more colors than those. With only 16 or 256 colors to choose from, Windows must select the closest match for the excess colors from its available palette.

18. Everything on my screen looks really greenish, bluish, or reddish. How do I fix this?

Check your Red-Green-Blue (RGB) adjustments.

1. On older monitors, look for small knobs on the monitor case.

2. On newer monitors, push the button on the monitor case which brings up the monitor's on-screen menu.

3. Push the selector buttons until you arrive at the color level settings. Most monitors will allow you to set the relative brightness of red, green, and blue dots on your tube.

No luck? Check your driver. Your computer likely has a video card which controls the display. It is controlled by special software called a driver. Each card/driver combination is a little different.

1. Click on the Start button, Settings, Control Panel, and the Display icon.

2. Click on the Settings tab.

3. Click on the Advanced button. You'll be shown a collection of tabs with settings, which adjust your display driver software. Look for settings, which adjust RGB levels.

4. If these tabs do not show driver information, click on the Start button, Settings, Control Panel, and then the System icon

5. Click on the Device Manager tab.

6. Click on the + (plus) sign next to Monitor.

7. Click on the monitor shown.

8. Click on the Properties button.

9. Click on the Drivers tab (if there is one).

10. See if you have or need a driver.

11. Click on Update Driver button if the dialog box says you need one and follow the instructions.

If you still have no luck, then your monitor may be dying a slow death. When you've exhausted all adjustment options, shut down your computer and borrow someone else's monitor for a little experiment:

1. Completely turn off your computer and monitor.

2. Disconnect the serial cable that runs to the back of your computer case.

3. Unplug the monitor's power cord. Remember which socket on your computer case takes the monitor's cable (you'll probably have only one choice that fits).

4. Bring over your test monitor and set it next to your original. Plug its serial cable into your computer case and plug it in.

5. Turn on the power to both your computer and the new monitor. If the borrowed monitor looks the same as your monitor, the problem might lie in your computer's video card. Call your Information Technology (IT) department, the manufacturer of your computer, or the store from which you bought the computer for help.

If the borrowed monitor looks good, take your monitor in for service or think about buying a new one. In our experience, the life of a monitor picture tube is four to six years.

Definitions:

Driver: A special piece of software designed to run a specific piece of hardware attached to your computer. Most drivers are provided by the hardware manufacturer and must be installed before the hardware can be used.

19. The icons and toolbars on my screen are too big (or too small). How do I change the size?

Most modern display devices will display at least 1,024x768 pixels. If you have an older display, it might only handle 800x600 pixels. The fewer the pixels your computer can use to display all your windows and icons, the bigger the icons will appear. To change them:

1. Click on the Start button, Settings, Control Panel, and then the Display icon.

2. Click on the Settings tab.

3. Go to the Desktop Area.

4. Set the slider to a higher setting. Windows will give you an opportunity to test out your settings before committing.

Your Windows screen font might be oversized. You can set the size of the fonts that Windows uses for icons and menus.

1. Click on the Start button, Settings, Control Panel, and then the Display icon

2. Click on the Appearance tab.

3. Click on the type of text that looks bad to you.

4. Select a new font size in the Size text box to the right of the Font text box.

TIP: Why bother? Select one of Windows' canned settings and forget about it. To avoid all this fancy finagling:

1. Click on the Start button, Settings, Control Panel, and the Display icon

2. Click on the Appearance tab.

3. Click on Schemes. You can select a collection of basic display properties.

TIP: Windows 98 users who want more complexity can:

1. Click on the Start button, Settings, Control Panel, and then the Display icon.

2. Click on the Appearance tab.

3. Click on Desktop Themes and select from a more varied package of sounds and images to decorate your desktop. You can expand your horizons by searching the Internet for free themes others have created for your entertainment.

20. My screen looks distorted or out of alignment. How do I fix this?

Your monitor is probably out of adjustment. Look on the front panel of your monitor. You should see some knobs or buttons. You'll be able to control the horizontal and vertical size of your screen image as well as the position of the image and pincushioning controls.

- Do you have a lot of empty black space around your screen image? Adjust the size of the image.

- Are you missing a piece of your screen image? Adjust the size or position of the image to see if something is being hidden off-screen.

- Do the sides of your image look curved? Try adjusting the pin-cushioning control to straighten up the edges.

Do you see a permanent ripple or wave on your screen?

- This is probably a job for a professional. You'll not be able to adjust this one.

Does your display seem to jiggle or vibrate?

1. Try running an extension cord to another outlet and hook up your computer and monitor to it. If the problem seems to disappear, you might be getting some power interference from another piece of equipment sharing your circuit.

2. Make sure your system isn't too close to fluorescent lighting of any kind.

3. On many video cards, you can adjust the refresh rate to best suit your specific monitor. Some monitors can handle very high rates and some cannot. If your refresh rate is set too high or too low, you might get a steady flickering on your screen. To adjust the refresh rate:

4. Click on the Start button, Settings, Control Panel, and then the Display icon.

5. Click on the Settings tab.

6. Click on the Advanced Properties button.

7. Look through the tabs for a refresh rate adjustment. If you can't adjust your refresh rate, think about trying another monitor. DO NOT change any other settings.

Definitions:

Pincushioning: A type of distortion that can be adjusted on some monitors. A monitor is pincushioning when the display appears to have curved sides.

Refresh rate: The frequency with which the monitor updates the display you see. This is usually expressed in Hertz (Hz). A flickering display may be caused by a refresh rate that's too low.

21. I can't see anything at all on my screen. What happened?

This is not good. If this is a desktop computer, the problem might be serious.

1. Make sure your monitor is actually plugged in and on. With modern power-saving features, it might be on Standby or Suspend mode. If you aren't sure, there's no harm in turning your monitor off and back on again. Also, try moving the mouse and tapping the shift keys to turn off any screen savers or power management features from Windows.

2. Try making sure your cable connection to your monitor is snug.

3. As a last resort, completely turn off both computer and monitor, wait a few seconds, and turn them back on again. If nothing happens this time, get some help.

If this is your laptop, don't panic.

1. Move your mouse and tap the shift keys to clear any active screensavers or power management features that might be shutting your display down.

2. Check to see if your computer is asleep or suspended. Usually a small light indicator will show you that the machine is not off but merely sleeping. You can reactivate it by touching a special key or hitting return. Give your machine a minute to respond before giving up and moving to the next step.

3. Look for a display setting key somewhere on the keyboard. Usually, laptops offer a key to switch between the power-draining onboard LCD display or an external monitor or both. If your machine is set to use only the external monitor, your screen might appear blank. Locate the key or button and push it once or twice to select your onboard screen.

Chapter 5
Windows
Operating
Systems

WINDOWS 95

1. I can't set up Windows 95. What can I do?

Do you have enough spare memory? Windows 95 setup needs at least 420 kilobytes (KB) free conventional memory, and you should have at least 3 megabytes (MB) of extended memory. To check how much you have:

1. Go to the DOS prompt.

2. Make sure you see only the hard drive prompt, usually C:\.

3. Type MEM (or mem).

4. Examine how much memory you have.

5. Type Exit (or, exit).

If you need more, consult with a technician, help desk support, or a computer guru who knows how to boost memory.

To be sure, you have an extended memory manager:

1. Go to the DOS prompt.

2. Make sure you see only the hard drive prompt, usually C:\.

3. Type Edit config.sys (or, edit config.sys). Make sure you have a space between Edit and config.sys.

4. You should see two lines. The first is DEVICE=C:\WIN-DOWS\HIMEM.SYS, the second is DOS=HIGH. You may or may not see the second line; the first line is more important.

5. If you don't see the lines, don't insert memory unless you know what you're doing. Consult with your technician, help desk support personnel, or computer.

TIP: Turn off any anti-virus programs before installing Windows. In fact, you may want to check for viruses before loading Windows. Or, install your virus software after you install Windows.

There are many possible Windows installation problems (because of the plethora of ways to configure and construct computers). We only list a few to look out for:

• Video driver conflicts

• Hardware detection problems

• INF files not properly installed

• Boot partition that cannot be located

• Corrupt or damaged installation CD-ROM or floppy disk

2.   My computer seems to be slowing down. What can I do?

Sadly, Windows is a memory hog; it's not efficient in disposing of useless files and data. You must do periodic housecleaning. Follow the steps below, in order, at least once every month, preferably twice.

• Delete all documents you've worked on. To do this:

1. Click on Start, Settings, and then Taskbar.

2. Click on Start Menu Programs tab.

3. Click on the Clear button so it's grayed out.

4. Click on the OK button.

- Delete all documents in your recycle bin. To do this:

    1. Double-click on the Recycle Bin icon (or click on Recycle Bin in Windows Explorer).

    2. Review all files in the bin to be sure you no longer need them.

    3. Click on the File drop-down menu (if you want to delete all files at once).

    4. Click on Empty Recycle Bin.

    5. Click on the OK button.

CAUTION: If you want to keep some of these files, transfer them to a disk or another folder within your hard drive before deleting files from the Recycle Bin. Do not leave important (even if temporary) files in your hard drive.

- Delete all temporary documents:

    1. Click on Start, Programs, Windows Explorer (unless, of course, you have created a shortcut icon for Windows Explorer).

    2. Click on the C:\ hard drive letter.

    3. Click on the Tools drop-down menu.

    4. Click and drag the mouse from Find to Files or Folders.

    5. Click on Files or Folders.

    6. In the Named text box, type *.tmp (the asterisk is a wildcard meaning any file).

7. Make sure that the C:\ hard drive is selected in the Look in text box.

8. Make sure you've checked the Include subfolders checkbox.

9. Click on the Find Now button.

10. Click on one of the files below.

11. Press Ctrl and the letter a (Ctrl+A). This action selects all files listed in the dialog box.

12. Press the Shift and Delete buttons (Shift+Del).

CAUTION: If you press the Delete button, the file is typically sent to the Recycle Bin, which gives you one more chance to save this document. If, however, you press Shift and then Delete, your file is completely deleted, gone, goodbye, adios. Don't use both buttons unless you're absolutely sure you don't need this file.

• Delete (or print and then delete) all the readme text files in your computer. Most software packages include up-to-date information in a readme text file that the company couldn't print in the accompanying documentation. Most of these files are useless; most can be deleted. The important ones can be printed and then deleted. To delete these files:

1. Click on the Start button, Programs, Windows Explorer (unless, of course, you have created a shortcut icon for Windows Explorer).

2. Click on the C:\ hard drive letter.

3. Click on the Tools drop-down menu.

4. Click and drag the mouse from Find to Files or Folders.

5. Click on Files or Folders.

6. In the Named text box, type readme.txt (make sure you put no spaces between readme, the period, and txt.

7. Make sure that the C:\ hard drive is selected in the Look in text box.

8. Make sure you've checked the Include subfolders checkbox.

9. Click on the Find Now button.

10. Double-click on each file and read it closely to determine if you want to print it, save it, or delete it. Some files may have gibberish or code in them; don't delete these until you're sure what they represent.

CAUTION: If you're not sure whether to delete a file, then DO NOT DELETE it. Simple enough, right? You have no idea how many people delete important files when they shouldn't have. Check with someone more knowledgeable before deleting anything.

- Delete all temporary Internet files. These text and graphics files can accumulate faster than you can say hello as you surf the Internet. To delete these files:

  1. Click on the Start button, Programs, Windows Explorer (unless you have a shortcut icon).

  2. Double-click on the Windows or Windows.000 folder.

  3. Click on the Temporary Internet Files folder.

  4. Click on one of the files in the right-hand window.

  5. Click on the Ctrl button and the letter a (Ctrl+A).

  6. Press the Shift and Delete buttons (Shift+Del). Before doing this, see the Caution above about what Shift+Del does.

- Delete all the files in the History folder. Not only do Internet files add up, each site's address is added in. To delete the history of where you've been:

  1. Click on the Start button, Programs, Windows Explorer (unless you've created a shortcut icon for Windows Explorer).

2. Double-click on the Windows or Windows.000 folder.

3. Click on the History folder.

4. Click on one of the files in the right-hand window.

5. Click on the Ctrl button and the letter a (Ctrl+A).

6. Press the Shift and Delete buttons (Shift+Del). Before doing this, see the Caution above about what Shift+Del does.

- If you've done all the above, run the Defragmentation (Defrag) utility. To run this utility, first make sure (make sure you first have screen savers and all other software packages are turned off). Then:

  1. Click on Start, Programs, Accessories, System Tools, and then Disk Defragmenter.

  2. Make sure the C:\ hard drive is selected.

  3. Click on the OK button. The system will check the hard drive and probably tell you that you don't need to defrag the drive; ignore this.

  4. Click on the Start button.

  5. Click on the Show Details button if you want to watch the Defrag proceedings.

CAUTION: You may get a message during the defrag process that you have bad data and must use ScanDisk first. If so, go to question four (below) for the ScanDisk procedure.

NOTE: If, after all of the above steps, your computer is still running slowly, you may need more RAM, a larger hard drive, or a more up-to-date operating system.

3. I don't have enough hard drive space. How can I increase it?

Do all the procedures described in question 2. If this isn't enough, consider buying a larger hard drive.

Do *not* compress the files with, for instance, the DriveSpace utility (especially don't' use DriveSpace with Banyan Vines networking). Many of these compression utilities compress all files indiscriminately. Many do not have adequate decompression processes: If you compress your drive and then want to undo the compression, you may find you cannot.

You can, however, use a ZIP utility to compress individual files. (As stated elsewhere, always save important files outside of the hard drive, whether on a floppy, a ZIP disk, or whatever, as insurance.) You can find many ZIP software packages on the Internet, for instance, at the *www.zdnet.com* location.

4. My software packages are acting weird. Should I use ScanDisk? How do I use it?

Quite possibly some files or programs are corrupted. One way around this problem is to uninstall and then reinstall the particular program. When problems begin, keep copious notes on what happens and when; this way, you may be able to detect a pattern.

- One way to prevent the hard drive from being weird is to use the ScanDisk utility. To do this, first make sure all screen savers and other software packages are turned off. Then:

  1. Click on Start, Programs, Accessories, System Tools, and then ScanDisk.

  2. Make sure the C:\ hard drive is selected.

  3. Click on the Standard button.

  4. Click on the Automatically fix errors checkbox.

  5. Click on the Start button.

- Another way to use ScanDisk is to do a more thorough cleansing of the data area:

  1. Click on Start, Programs, Accessories, System Tools, and then ScanDisk.

  2. Make sure the C:\ hard drive is selected.

  3. Click on the Thorough button.

  4. Click on the Options button.

  5. Click on the Data area only button. (Make sure both checkboxes below are unchecked.)

  6. Click on the Automatically fix errors checkbox.

  7. Click on the Start button.

- A third way to use ScanDisk is to do a thorough cleansing of the system area:

  1. Click on Start, Programs, Accessories, System Tools, and then ScanDisk.

  2. Make sure the C:\ hard drive is selected.

  3. Click on the Thorough button.

  4. Click on the Options button.

  5. Click on the System area only button. (Make sure both checkboxes below are unchecked.)

  6. Click on the Automatically fix errors checkbox.

  7. Click on the Start button.

CAUTION: Do not save any important files only in your hard drive. In fact, do not trust your hard drive. Why not? All hard drives will eventually die, without much warning. In fact, save all important on *two* floppies, ZIP disks, etc. Portable media also can die.

NOTE: Set your software to save your documents every three minutes to ensure that you don't lose much information or effort if the system crashes. To set software saving time in Word (some software packages don't allow this):

1. Open the Word software package.

2. Click on the Tools drop-down menu.

3. Click on Options, which opens the Options dialog box.

4. Click on the Save tab.

5. Check the Automatic Save Every checkbox.

6. Adjust the time limit in the box to the right of the checkbox.

5. I want to change the way the desktop looks. How do I do it?

Many people want to change the desktop, for many reasons. Some make the icons larger to see them more easily; others want to move the icons into certain groupings. Still others want to add a varied background or pictures of their family. We will discuss all of these.

• To change the background of the desktop:

1. Right-click anywhere on the desktop (but not on top of an icon).

2. Select Properties, which opens the Display Properties dialog box.

3. Click on the Background tab.

4. Select one of the patterns in the left-hand box.

5. Click on the Apply button to see if you like the pattern. (If you have tiled Wallpaper, you won't see any pattern, because Wallpaper has precedence over Patterns.)

• To customize the background design of the desktop:

1. Right-click anywhere on the desktop (but not on top of an icon).

2. Select Properties, which opens the Display Properties dialog box.

3. Click on the Background tab.

4. Select one of the patterns in the left-hand box.

5. Click on the Edit Pattern button (the pattern will appear in the Pattern Editor dialog box).

6. Click inside the Pattern Editor to change the design.

7. Change the name of your new pattern (in case you want the original back).

8. Click on the Done button.

9. Click on the Apply button to see if you like the pattern. (If you have tiled Wallpaper, you won't see any pattern, because Wallpaper has precedence over Patterns.)

• To change the wallpaper of your desktop:

1. Right-click anywhere on the desktop (but not on top of an icon).

2. Select Properties, which opens the Display Properties dialog box.

3. Click on the Background tab.

4. Select one of the wallpapers in the left-hand box.

5. Click on the Tile button if you want the wallpaper to fill the screen.

6. Click on the Center button if you want the wallpaper (or, Internet image) to be in the center of the desktop. Some people scan pictures of their family, et al., and then center them in the desktop with a pattern behind. This is how you do it:

7. Click on the Apply button to see if you like the wallpaper. (If you choose to tile Wallpaper, you will no longer see any Pattern you may have chosen.)

CAUTION: Even though many wallpaper designs may look interesting, be wary of using complicated ones. For instance, the bubbles design may look fun, but you can't see your icons well over this design.

- To add a picture/graphic from the World Wide Web:

1. Find the image/graphic you want.

2. Right-click on the image.

3. Select the option to save the image as wallpaper.

4. Right-click anywhere on the desktop (but not on top of an icon).

5. Select Properties, which opens the Display Properties dialog box.

6. Click on the Background tab.

7. Select Netscape wallpaper (or Internet Explorer wallpaper) in the left-hand box.

8. Click on the Tile button if you want the wallpaper to fill the screen.

9. Click on the Center button if want the wallpaper you saved to be in the center of the desktop. People scan pictures of their family, et al., and then center them in their desktop with a pattern behind. This is how you do it:

10. Click on the Apply button to see if you like the wallpaper. (If you choose to tile Wallpaper, you will no longer see any Pattern you may have chosen.)

• To change, add, or turn off a screen saver:

1. Right-click anywhere on the desktop (but not on top of an icon).

2. Select Properties, which opens the Display Properties dialog box.

3. Click on the Screen Saver tab.

4. Click on the drop-down arrow under the Screen Saver heading.

5. Select one of the screen savers or None, if you want to turn off the screen saver.

6. Click on the Settings button.

CAUTION: Do not add a password to your screen saver. If, for instance, you set a password, go to lunch, and then forget your password, you will not be able to get into your computer unless you turn it off and then back on. How many passwords do you really need?

• To change the size of your desktop icons:

1. Right-click anywhere on the desktop (but not on top of an icon).

2. Select Properties, which opens the Display Properties dialog box.

3. Click on the Appearance tab.

4. Click on the drop-down arrow to the right of the Item text box.

5. Click on and select Icon.

6. Adjust size (number) to the right of the text box. Adjust the number by small amounts because you don't need much of a numerical change to make a big change on the desktop.

- To smooth the edges of your icons:

    1. Right-click anywhere on the desktop (but not on top of an icon).

    2. Select Properties, which opens the Display Properties dialog box.

    3. Click on the Plus tab.

    4. Click on the Smooth edges of screen fonts checkbox.

- To change the look of components of your desktop:

    1. Right-click anywhere on the desktop (but not on top of an icon).

    2. Select Properties, which opens the Display Properties dialog box.

    3. Click on the Appearance tab.

    4. Click on any of the components just below the Appearance tab, or click on the drop-down arrow under the Item selection.

    5. Click on the component.

    6. Adjust the color and/or size. Remember not to make wild changes. Adjust amounts by small amounts because you don't need much of a numerical change to make a big change on the desktop.

NOTE: If you click on the drop-down arrow of the Color box, you can click on the lowest button, which will allow you to customize the colors to your heart's content. The more resolution your monitor has, the more you will see the subtle gradations in color.

- To change the resolution of the monitor:

    1. Right-click anywhere on the desktop (but not on top of an icon).

    2. Select Properties, which opens the Display Properties dialog box.

3. Click on the Settings tab.

4. Click and drag the slider under the Desktop area to increase the resolution.

5. Also, click on the drop-down arrow under the Color palette area.

6. Select the highest resolution.

CAUTION: As you raise the resolution under the Desktop area, you also reduce the size of the screen. Increased resolution is a tradeoff. Luckily, if you change the resolution, you can always change it back.

6. I have an application that appears when I click on my Start button list. I don't want it there. How do I get rid of it?

A lot of applications insinuate themselves here. To delete them, do the following:

1. Click on Start, Settings, and then Taskbar.

2. Click on the Start Menu Programs tab.

3. Click on the Remove button.

4. Scroll all the way to the bottom.

5. Click on the application you wish to remove from the Start button list.

6. Click on Remove.

7. Click on Close.

7. How do I change the time and date in my desktop?

• To change the time and date:

1. Right-click on the time showing in the bottom right-hand corner (on the right side of the taskbar). This opens the Adjust Date/Time dialog box.

2. Click on the Date & Time tab or on the Time Zone tab.

3. Adjust.

4. Make sure you've checked the Automatically adjust clock for daylight savings changes checkbox (in the Time Zone tab).

- If you don't see the clock in the lower right-hand corner of your desktop and you want to change the time and date:

    1. Click on Start, Settings, Control Panel, and then the Date/Time icon.

    2. Click on the Date & Time tab or on the Time Zone tab.

    3. Adjust.

    4. Make sure you've checked the Automatically adjust clock for daylight savings changes checkbox (in the Time Zone tab).

8. What are some keyboard shortcuts in the desktop I should know?

Some of the keyboard shortcuts on the desktop (not in your applications) are:

F1	=	Help
F3	=	Find
F5	=	Refresh (you may not see anything change)
F6	=	Alternates between the Start button and the last selected icon
Ctrl+a	=	Selects all icons on the desktop
Alt+s	=	Opens the Start button

Alt+F4   =   Opens the Shut Down Windows dialog box

Alt+Tab   =   Opens an application or allows you to switch between open
               applications

NOTE: As with other functions, the commands may be different on your
computer depending on the version and type of its operating system, the
available software, etc. On the desktop, go to Help and find keyboard
shortcuts for an up-to-date list for your computer.

9. What are some of the keyboard shortcuts within applications that I should know?

F1   =   Help (in Excel)

F2   =   Insert in a cell (in Excel)

F3   =   Help (in Word; not in Excel)

F4   =   Repeats last command

F5   =   Find

F5   =   GoTo (in Excel)

F7   =   Spellcheck (in Excel and Word)

F8   =   Activates the Extend property (in Excel and Word); Esc
               button turns F8 off

F11   =   Opens a Chart folder (in Excel)

F12   =   Activates the Save As dialog box

Ctrl+b   =   Activates or deactivates the Bold button (in Excel and
               Word)

Ctrl+e   =   Activates the Centering button (in Word)

Ctrl+f   =   Opens the Find dialog box (in Excel)

Ctrl+f   =   Opens the Find tab in the Find and Replace dialog box (in
               Word)

Ctrl+g   =   Opens the Go To dialog box (in Excel and Word)

Ctrl+h   =   Opens the Replace dialog box (in Excel and Word)

Ctrl+i   =   Activates or deactivates the Italics button (in Excel and
               Word)

Ctrl+k	=	Saves your document before creating a hyperlink (in Excel)
Ctrl+o	=	Opens the Open dialog box
Ctrl+p	=	Opens the Print dialog box
Ctrl+s	=	Opens the Save dialog box
Ctrl+u	=	Activates or deactivates the Underline button (in Excel and Word)
Ctrl+w	=	Allows you to save changes to your current document
Ctrl+y	=	Activates the Redo command
Ctrl+z	=	Activates the Undo command
Ctrl+Tab	=	Alternates between tabs in an open dialog box

NOTE: Many applications have other keyboard functions and new versions of software packages sometimes change keyboard functions.

To find the keyboard shortcuts in your software applications:

1. Click on the Help drop-down menu (in the application).

2. Click on Contents and Index.

3. Click on the Find tab.

4. Type in two words: keyboard shortcut (do not capitalize either word).

5. Select the Shortcut keys topic (or, some similar title).

WINDOWS 98: CHANGES/UPDATES

One difference from Windows 95 to Windows 98 is the change in disk storage from FAT16 to FAT32 and a better anti-virus program. Naturally, more bugs have been worked out, but then newer bugs have been introduced. Still, people who have to upgrade have more problems compared to those who buy a system with a pre-installed Windows 98 system.

Prepare for problems by having all information handy (serial numbers, software packages installed, and all other pertinent information) along with all phone numbers when calling Microsoft, a third party, or the company you bought the computer and/or software from.

Another major change is the ability to get onto the Web quickly, preferably through Microsoft's Internet Explorer. For instance, in the Display Properties dialog box, you'll see a Web tab in addition to the usual roster of Background, Screen Saver, etc.

The Taskbar includes a Quick Launch area for programs you need with a simple click or double-click. The Start Button list includes a Log Off function for those in a network.

Windows 98 now has Outlook Express to manage and sort e-mail and newsgroup information. You can create folders for subjects, etc., to make your life easier.

To keep Windows 98 running smoothly, you can use System File Checker, designed to verify the integrity of the files in the operating system, which was difficult in the Windows 95 operating system. System File Checker will allow you to see whether corrupt files exist.

ScanDisk has not changed at all, but the Defrag utility has been improved with a more efficient rewrite/organizational capability.

Hardware device conflicts are most usually resolved by removing the opposing driver. To find a driver problem/conflict in Windows 98:

1. Have your installation floppy disk or CD-ROM available.

2. Click on the Start button, Settings, and then Control Panel.

3. Click on the System icon.

4. Click on the Device Manager tab.

5. Click on the + sign next to the hardware having the problem.

6. Click on the appropriate hardware under the hardware category you have selected.

7. Click on the Properties button

8. Click on the General or Driver tabs to see if a conflict exists.

9. If a conflict exists, try the Update button.

If you're having problems with all the confusing choices during installation of software packages, consider using the Version Conflict Manager (VCM), which runs during setup. The VCM allows you to choose which Dynamic Link Library (DLL) version you want to keep when a conflict occurs. To get to the VCM:

1. Click on Start, Programs, Accessories, and then System Tools.

2. Click on System Information, Tools, and then Version Conflict Manager.

The Windows Report tool lets you collect information on a bug in the Windows system. The Collected Information command area is the first place to stop to examine your system.

Also included is the System Configuration Utility, which provides control and advanced troubleshooting. You have to teach the system when you want to purge the Recycle Bin and how much free space you feel you need (not what the software considers appropriate).

Some of the big incompatibilities are between hardware and software. Other categories of problems include corrupt files and user error. As always, check all cables, connections, etc., and restart the computer to see if this will clear the problem.

If you need more information about Windows 98, you can consult its Microsoft System Information (MSI) tool. The MSI will have certain important categories to examine, such as Conflicts/Sharing, Problem Devices, and more. To get to the MSI:

1. Click on Start, Programs, Accessories, and then Systems Tools.

2. You can also find this file in Windows Explorer by searching for the MSINFO32.EXE file.

The most common problem after installation is a system crash. A Windows 98 crash should be first checked with ScanDisk, the MSI, through Device Manager, etc. Also, run your anti-virus software. At worst, you may have to re-install Windows 98.

Other conflicts could be drivers too old to operate, such as an older and slower display adapter, or some drivers from software packages.

Definitions:

Dynamic Link Library (DLL): A Microsoft library of stored routines used by software packages. You can find them in Windows Explorer by looking for the .dll extension.

Chapter 6*
Ergonomics

Ergonomics is a phrase that you have probably heard many times, but not really sure what it is? It is used to sell cars, kitchen appliances, cellular phones, computer keyboards, and mice. So, what is it?

Ergonomics is the design of the workplace that takes into consideration human's physical, physiological, biomechanical, and psychological capabilities. In addition to these fields, ergonomics also includes the engineering, biomechanics, and physiology.

So, what do all of these fields have to do with ergonomics? Quite simply, product designers look at a tool, device or situation and ask two questions: For whom was it designed and for what task was it designed?

They then analyze the human body and recommend ways to reduce as much stress on the body as possible. Therefore, ergonomically designed means the seat, table, etc., is designed to accommodate the body properly.

Given the general acceptance of ergonomics and that it reduces worker injury, there are no current laws governing workplace ergonomics. However, the Occupational Safety and Health Administration (OSHA) is pushing for one and has submitted its recommendations for creating one. You can find it and other ergonomic issues on OSHA's Web site: *http://www.osha-slc.gov/ergonomics-standard/index.html.*

*These answers are meant to guide you in solving your physical pain or problems. These answers are not meant to be medical answers for your specific problems. You may want to consult a specialist, such as a chiropractor.

IS YOUR CHAIR RIGHT FOR YOU?

1. I work long hours at my computer and no matter what I do, I just cannot get comfortable. Any suggestions?

First, you should examine the type of chair that you are using. It will fall into one of the four basic classifications of office chairs: task chair, manager's chair, executive chair, or side/stack chair.

* The Task Chair (a.k.a.: stenographer or secretary chairs) comes in a wide range of features and controls. This is your basic computer work chair. It is usually inexpensive and designed for receptionists and "budget conscience" environments. For heavy computer work you will want a task chair that fulfills these three minimum requirements:

    1. Seat moves up and down

    2. Seat tilts forward towards the keyboard (either just the seat, or the entire chair)

    3. Arm height is adjustable up and down, although width adjustments is recommended

* The Manager's Chair or Multiple-task (multi-purpose) Chair is designed for individuals who perform a wide array of tasks that include the following:

    1. Typing on the keyboard

    2. Holding meetings in the office

    3. Talking on the phone

* The Executive Chair is a big, cushy chair almost feels like your living room chair and is designed for individuals who hold meetings in their office, read, answer e-mail, or talk on the phone. This chair features the following two characteristics:

1. Mid to high back

2. Limited controls: seat moves up and down and the chair may recline

CAUTION: The Executive Chair is not designed for long-term use in front of a computer and should not be used for heavy computer work.

- The Side/Stack or Guest Chair allows for no adjustments designed for sitting for short periods of time. This chair is not recommended for doing heavy computer work and is usually the uncomfortable chair that you sit in at meetings and conferences.

- If you sit at a computer for more than four hours, you should be using a task chair. Under no circumstances should you do any type of computer work in a side/stack chair, kitchen chair, dining room chair, rocking chair or any other type of chair that is not adjustable! In addition do not work at your laptop computer while in bed; you body will not be supported properly.

2. I'm sitting in the correct chair, but I still cannot get comfortable. Any suggestions?

Your chair probably needs to be adjusted properly. Refer to the chair adjustment chart on page **xxx** to ensure maximum comfort.

3. My chair is perfectly adjusted, but I still cannot get comfortable. Is there something wrong with me?

Probably not. Your chair is not the only object that should be adjusted. Other factors such as keyboard, mouse and monitor position also contribute to you comfort. Refer to the workstation adjustment chart to ensure maximum comfort. You may want to note the four following considerations:

- Adding an adjustable keyboard and mouse tray to your desk

- Purchasing a document holder

- Moving your monitor closer to you

- Eliminating bending over for files or drawers from your chair

4. My eyes hurt after several hours of looking at my monitor. Could the problem be radiation emitting from it?

Most likely no. Most computer monitors manufactured within the past ten years do not emit any form of radiation. If you monitor is older than ten years, it may be time to get a new one. Older monitors were not constructed by the same standards as today and many do not meet current energy or safety regulations. Refer to the next question of this section if you are experiencing any other problems while working with your computer.

5. After working at my computer I often experience headaches, eyestrain, itching and burning eyes, and/or double vision. What could be the cause of this?

One or a combination of several factors could be the cause. Refer to the questions following these factors:

- Computer monitor

- Improper monitor settings

- Room lighting

- Poor air quality

6. Could my computer monitor or Video Display Terminal (VDT) be causing the problems in Question Five?

Older monitors (as well as some inexpensive "bargain" monitors) may not be up to today's standards. These monitors can contain some characteristics that could cause eye irritation.

- *Flicker:* Flicker occurs when the monitor does not refresh itself as quickly as it should or once did. A monitor works by using an internal light beam that scans the monitor from top to bottom. This is called the refresh rate. Monitors manufactured today will have a refresh rate of at least 75 Hertz (Hz) for monitor resolutions up to 1,280 by 1,024 pixels. Some monitors may have a faster rate. For monitors larger than 1,280 by 1,024 pixels and up to 1,600 by 1,200 pixels, a refresh rate of 60 Hz is acceptable.

- *Brightness:* Overly bright or overly dim monitors may cause eye problems. Adjust the brightness on your monitor so that it is bright enough to show the image but not radiating light as if it were a lamp.

- *Fuzziness:* Many monitors look fuzzy because they have too high of a bit depth. This means that the dots that makeup the picture are too large which makes a monitor look fuzzy, blurry, or out of focus. Monitors should have a picture tube bit depth, or aperture grille pitch of 0.28 or lower. This is usually listed on the monitor specifications as the dot pitch. The smaller the number means more dots will make up your picture and result in a clearer, sharper image.

- *Color:* Incorrect colors, greenish (or other color) tint, or even black or dark blue backgrounds with white text can cause the eye to become irritated. If the colors on your monitor are washed out, dull or faded, you may need a new monitor.

7. Could an improper monitor setting be causing the problems in Question Five?

Yes. Most people never adjust their monitor. In most cases, it can be too bright or too dim. Some monitors have a built-in calibration allowing you to adjust the settings properly, while others may have a guide. The Apple Macintosh offers built-in software calibration through the Color Sync control panel. Owners of Windows-based PCs should refer to their operations manuals for more information on how to calibrate their monitors properly.

8.   Could improper lighting be causing the problems in Question Five?

Poorly lit environments can also cause eye problems. Does one of these situations apply to you?

*   Bright backgrounds and dark foregrounds (or vice-versa): When taking a picture if you have a bright source of light surrounded by darker objects, the camera will adjust itself to the bright source and everything in the background will be dark. Your eyes work in this way as well. The following three situations can cause eye problems:

    1. Too much light in the work area: Is your room excessively bright? Do you have a window behind you that constantly reflects light on your monitor? Or, does your monitor have an intense light behind it such as a window?

    2. Too little light in the work area: It is not good for your eyes to work in the dark with no other light than the glow of your monitor. You should always supplement your monitor with an additional light source. A desk lamp with a dimmer control will compliment your monitor by spreading light over your work area.

    3. Monitor glare: If you see your reflection, or your surroundings, in your monitor while it is on you should consider purchasing a glare guard. Many times people have problems with glare on their monitor and do not even know it. In many cases, the problem goes unnoticed and the result is headaches or eye problems.

CAUTION: In all three of these situations the intense light will cause your eyes to strain as they try to adjust and compensate for the varying degrees of light density. All of this activity by the eye can result in a headache.

9.   Could poor air quality be causing the problems in Question Five?

Low humidity and dry air can cause skin dryness and eye irritation. In addition, low humidity can cause dust and lint to form around your computer monitor and irritate the eyes. Here are some suggestions to improve the air quality in your work environment:

- Work in a room that has good air circulation and is well ventilated

- Humidity should be between 30 percent and 60 percent

- If you work in a cubical environment the partitions should be six inches off the floor to improve air circulation

- Clean the air vents and change the filter in your furnace or air conditioner once a month

- Ducts should be cleaned every one to three years depending on your environment

- Dust your monitor and computer at least once a week

NOTE: Also remember to adjust your room lighting, blink your eyes often, take breaks and walk around (at least every twenty minutes), get an eye exam, and/or have an air quality check. Pollutants or dust in the air that causes eye irritation.

10. My body aches after working at my computer. What could possibly cause this?

It really depends on what part of your body is hurting. The following four areas will be examined in more detail:

1. Neck

2. Shoulders

3. Upper back

4. Arms, elbows, wrists, and hands

The following sections represent the area of the body where you may be experiencing pain. Because some of the symptoms may pertain to more than one injury, review all of the symptoms for each injury under the section titled "What does it feel like?"

NOTE: This book is not a substitute, or replacement of trained medical advice. If you are experiencing any of these symptoms, you should consult a licensed physician.

11. My neck aches. What are some factors that could cause this?

* Tension Neck Syndrome

  What does it feel like?
  1. Irritation of a group of muscles in the neck.
  2. Reduced range of motion in the neck.

  What can cause this?
  1. Working with neck bent forward or backward, e.g., when looking at a computer monitor.

  Possible courses of action:
  1. In many circumstances, people put their monitor on top of their desktop computer. This is not good because it usually raises the monitor too high above eye level. The top of the monitor should be just below eye level. Refer the workstation adjustment chart for more information.

* General Neck Pain

  What does it feel like?
  1. Pain in the back and sides of the neck.

  What can cause this?
  1. Maintaining a twisted neck posture, e.g., from working with a monitor and/or reference documents.
  2. Having the neck bent to one side, e.g., from holding the phone with one shoulder.

  Possible courses of action:
  1. In many circumstances, people put their monitor on top of their desktop computer. This is not a good thing because it makes the monitor too high to adjust properly. Your monitor should be just below eye level. Refer to the chair adjustment chart and then proceed to the workstation adjustment chart.

2. If you talk on the phone for long periods of time, or if you enter information into the computer while talking on the phone use a telephone headset.

12. My shoulders ache. What is causing this?

*   Tendinitis of the Shoulder (Rotator Cuff Syndrome)

    What does it feel like?
    1. Dull and persistent ache in the shoulder region; pain can extend into arms.

    What can cause this?
    1. Working with the hand above the shoulder; regularly carrying loads on the shoulder like carrying luggage with a shoulder strap or throwing objects such as a baseball pitcher.
    2. Working with elbows elevated (e.g. typing on a work surface that is too high).

    Possible courses of action:
    1. If you work at a desk adjust your chair and then adjust your workstation.
    2. If you travel and carry briefcases, packages, luggage, or other items, you should alternate between carrying these items with your left hand, and then your right. Do this frequently to avoid fatigue in one arm.
    3. If you work in a mailroom or another area where you are often working with your hands over your head then use a stool or a ladder instead of reaching over your head.
    4. Consult your physician.

*   Thoracic Outlet Syndrome

    What does it feel like?
    1. Tingling in the fingertips, including numbness and pain in the hands and arms. (Symptoms parallel Carpal Tunnel Syndrome, but are caused by shoulder/upper arm problems.)

    What can cause this?
    1. Continuously reaching overhead.

2. Working for long periods in a posture that restricts upper body movement.
3. Carrying loads in the hand, or lugging loads around using a shoulder strap (e.g., carrying a suit bag for long periods).

Possible courses of action:
1. If you work at a desk, adjust your chair and then adjust your workstation.
2. If you travel and carry briefcases, packages, luggage, or other items, you should alternate carrying them between your left and right hand to avoid fatigue in one arm.
3. If you work in a mailroom or another area where you are often working with your hands over your head, then use a stool or a ladder instead of reaching over your head.
4. Consult your physician.

- Lower Back Pain

What does it feel like?
1. A painful sensation in the low back area

What can cause this?
1. Bending your back forward, resulting in an unnatural spinal curve (e.g., from sitting in a chair with a seat pan that is flat or sloped backward).
2. Prolonged sitting with unsupported posture.
3. Twisting, e.g., when retrieving reference materials.

Possible courses of action:
1. When lifting heavy items, use your legs.
2. If you are getting something out of a bottom drawer, kneel or crouch to retrieve it, but do not bend over.
3. While sitting in your chair, get out of your chair to get files and items that have fallen on the floor.
4. When reaching for an item across your desk, do not. Get up to retrieve it or move it closer to you.
5. Consult your physician.

13. My arms, elbows, wrists, and/or hands ache. What may be causing this?

- Cubital Tunnel Syndrome

  What does it feel like?
  1. Tingling, numbness, or pain radiating into the ring and little fingers.

  What can cause this?
  1. Resting forearm near elbow on a sharp edge (e.g., from typing with forearms resting against a hard-edged table).
  2. Working with the elbows bent less than 90 degrees (e.g., from typing on a keyboard that is too high).
  3. Compression of the ulnar nerve (located below the notch of the elbow).

  Possible courses of action:
  1. Add an adjustable keyboard and mouse tray to your workstation.
  2. Add a wrist rest to your keyboard.
  3. Purchase an ergonomic keyboard.
  4. Consult your physician.

- Tendinitis of the Elbow (also called epicondylitis, tennis elbow, and golfers' elbow).

  What does it feel like?
  1. Irritation of the tendon attached to the elbow.

  What can cause this?
  1. Resting forearm near elbow on a sharp edge (e.g., from typing with forearms resting against a hard-edged table).
  2. Turning screws or small parts.
  3. Playing a musical instrument, playing tennis, pitching or bowling.

  Possible courses of action:
  1. Add an adjustable keyboard and mouse tray to your workstation.
  2. Add a wrist rest to your keyboard.
  3. Purchase an ergonomic keyboard.
  4. Take frequent breaks.

5. Stretch.
6. Consult your physician.

- Tendinitis of the Wrist

  What does it feel like?
  1. Pain in the wrist, especially on the outer edges of the hand.

  What can cause this?
  1. Forceful bending of the wrist forward and backward.

  Possible courses of action:
  1. Add an adjustable keyboard and mouse tray to your workstation.
  2. Add a wrist rest to your keyboard.
  3. Purchase an ergonomic keyboard.
  4. Take frequent breaks.
  5. Stretch.
  6. Consult your physician.

- Ganglionic Cyst

  What does it feel like?
  1. Bump on the wrist or hand, that is sore and tender when touched.

  What can cause this?
  1. Pressure from repeated pushing or turning action involving the wrist; forceful handwriting.

  Possible courses of action:
  1. Add an adjustable keyboard and mouse tray to your workstation.
  2. Add a wrist rest to your keyboard.
  3. Purchase an ergonomic keyboard.
  4. Take frequent breaks.
  5. Stretch.
  6. Consult your physician.

- De Quervain's Disease

  What does it feel like?
  1. Pain in the tendon of the thumb.

What can cause this?
1. Poor mouse placement.
2. Prolonged thumb extension (e.g., from not using thumb while typing).
3. High repetition with force (e.g., from typing with excessive force).
4. Forcefully extending the hand backward or to the side.
5. Rapidly rotating the hand.

Possible courses of action:
1. Add an adjustable keyboard and mouse tray to your workstation.
2. Add a wrist rest to your keyboard.
3. Purchase an ergonomic keyboard.
4. Take frequent breaks.
5. Stretch.
6. Consult your physician.

• Carpal Tunnel Syndrome (CTS)

What does it feel like?
1. Tingling in the fingertips often followed by numbness and pain in the hands, it can include a vise-like pressure on the wrists.
2. Pressure can send shocks of pain throughout the forearm and upper arm, extending in severe cases to the shoulder.
3. Over time, patients suffering from CTS lose grip strength and hand/wrist/arm range of motion.

What can cause this?
1. Compression of the median nerve as it passes through the carpal tunnel in the wrist.
2. Repetitive motion of the wrist, especially fully extending the hand toward the forearm or away from the forearm.
3. Repeatedly bending the wrist to either side; pinch-gripping a tool or device.
4. High repetition with force (e.g., typing with excessive force).

Possible courses of action:
1. Add an adjustable keyboard and mouse tray to your workstation.
2. Add a wrist rest to your keyboard.

3. Purchase an ergonomic keyboard.
4. Take frequent breaks.
5. Stretch.
6. Consult your physician.

- Tenosynovitis

What does it feel like?
1. Swelling of the sheath, which covers a tendon that leads to irritation. Often found in hands and shoulders, but can occur wherever tendons are located.

What can cause this?
1. Repeated wrist motions, forcefully extending the hand backward or to the side; rapidly rotating the hand.
2. Extreme wrist flexion or extension, e.g., from typing with the wrist on a work surface with fingers arched.

Possible courses of action:
1. Add an adjustable keyboard and mouse tray to your workstation.
2. Add a wrist rest to your keyboard.
3. Purchase an ergonomic keyboard.
4. Take frequent breaks.
5. Stretch.
6. Consult your physician.

- Trigger Finger

What does it feel like?
1. Tendon becomes nearly locked; finger motion becomes jerky, sometimes with an audible pop.

What can cause this?
1. Repetitive motion of a finger, or fingers, in which the end segment of finger is flexed, while middle segments are straight.

Possible courses of action:
1. Add an adjustable keyboard and mouse tray to your workstation.
2. Add a wrist rest to your keyboard.
3. Purchase an ergonomic keyboard.
4. Take frequent breaks.
5. Stretch.
6. Consult your physician.

Definitions:

Carpal Tunnel Syndrome (CTS): CTS is generally attributed to compression of the median nerve as it passes through the carpal tunnel in the wrist. Workers at risk for CTS include anyone who performs repeated manual operations involving the hand and wrist or using a computer keyboard and mouse with an awkward risk posture.

Cubital Tunnel Syndrome: Caused by working with the elbows bent at 90 degrees for long periods of time; such as when working on a computer. Symptoms include loss of sensation, numbness, tingling and muscle wasting in the pinky and ring fingers.

De Quervain's Disease: Caused by wrist, forearm and thumb being in an awkward position or motion for long periods of time. Causes inflammation of the tendon sheaths located at the base of the thumb.

Occupational Safety and Health Administration (OSHA): Government agency whose job is to protect employees from harm or death due to hazardous or unsafe working environments.

Rotator Cuff Syndrome: Caused by excessive should vibration that could be due to extended flexing of the arm or vibration. Symptoms include restricted should movement and pain.

Tendinitis: Caused by repetitive stress or force in the hands or arms. Symptoms occur when tendons in the hand, elbow, or shoulder become sore and inflamed, causing tenderness, swelling and pain in the hand or arm.

Tenosynovitis: Caused by repetitive hand, wrist or forearm movement such as typing. Symptoms include tenderness, swelling and pain of the hand, wrist or forearm.

Thoracic Outlet Syndrome: Caused by repetitive overhead extension of the shoulders, arms, or hands. Symptoms include pain at the base of the neck or in the shoulder, arm, or hand.

Trigger Finger: Caused by a cyst in the tendon sheath. Symptoms include locking of the finger in a bent position accompanied by pain.

APPENDIX I: WORK SURFACE ADJUSTMENT CHART

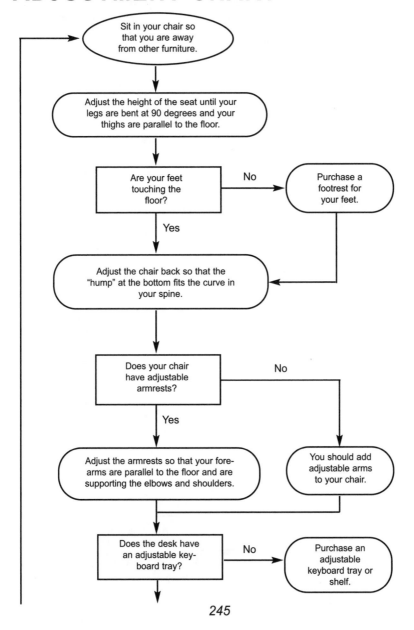

Sit in your chair so that you are away from other furniture.

Adjust the height of the seat until your legs are bent at 90 degrees and your thighs are parallel to the floor.

Are your feet touching the floor?

No → Purchase a footrest for your feet.

Yes

Adjust the chair back so that the "hump" at the bottom fits the curve in your spine.

Does your chair have adjustable armrests?

No

Yes

Adjust the armrests so that your fore-arms are parallel to the floor and are supporting the elbows and shoulders.

You should add adjustable arms to your chair.

Does the desk have an adjustable key-board tray?

No → Purchase an adjustable keyboard tray or shelf.

245

Work Surface Adjustment Chart, *cont'd.*

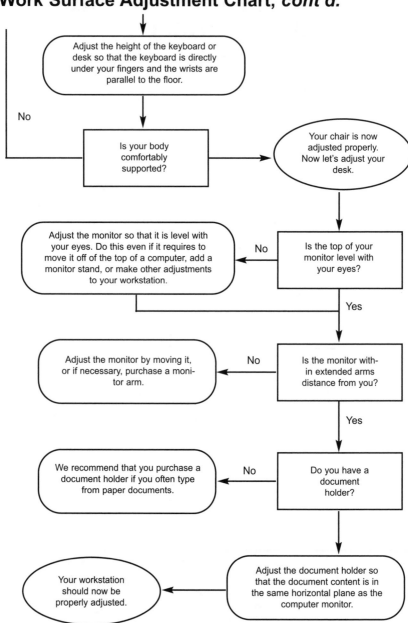

Appendix II
Addresses

Note: These addresses, phone numbers, and sites were active at the time of publication. They may have closed, altered addresses, etc., so you may have to use a search engine to find the particular company. Please also understand that just because we are listing a company does not constitute an endorsement.

HARDWARE (COMPUTER SYSTEMS)

www.aberdeeninc.com (desktops/tech. info.)
Aberdeen, Inc.
800-501-9218 //800-502-6502

www.acer.com
Acer America Corp.
800-551-2237

www.accessmicro.com (almost 50,000 items)

www.applemacnet.com (Apple, PC, etc.)

www.athome.compaq.com (888-628-2828): Compaq computers

www.axissys.com (computer systems)
Axis Systems
1134 N. Gilbert Street
Anaheim, CA 92801
800-378-9014

www.blackbox.com (cabling/networks)

www.buyabs.com
American Business Services
9997 East Rose Hills Road, Whittier, CA 90601
800.876.8088

www.buy-atlas.com (computer systems)
Atlas Micro Logistic, Inc.
1302 John Reed Court, City of Industry, CA 91745
800-336-6898

www.buycomp.com (hardware/networks)

www.cdw.com (computers)
CDW Computer Centers
200 N. Milwaukee Ave., Vernon Hills, IL 60061
800-279-4239

www.chilipepperpc.com

www.compdirect.com
Comp Direct
417 Fifth Ave., New York City, NY 10016
800-931-7070 // 212-696-4777

www.computer411.com (discontinued/overstocked PCs)

www.computergate.com (systems)
Computergate International
2960 Gordon Ave., Santa Clara, CA 95051
888-437-0895

www.crucial.com (memory modules)
888-363-2563

www.cybermaxpc.com
CyberMax Computer, Inc.
133 N. 5th St., Allentown, PA 18102
800-443-9868 // 610-770-1808

www.cyberpowerinc.com
CyberPower, Inc.
4802 Little John St., Baldwin Park, CA 91706
800-707-0393 // 626-813-7730

www.cyberwarehouse.com (notebooks, PCs)
CyberWarehouse
800-792-2923

www.damark.com (discontinued computers)

www.dell.com // *www.dell4me.com*
Dell Computers
800-241-5864 // 800-436-9102
800-241-2095 // 800-626-4395

www.directplus.compaq.com (Compaq computers)

www.fpcdirect.fujitsu-pc.com (laptops)

www.fujitsu-pc.com (laptops)
877-372-3473

www.gateway.com
Gateway Computers
800-555-2073

www.harmonycomputers.com (laptops, etc.)
Harmony Computers
1801 Flatbush Ave., Brooklyn, NY 11210
800-870-1663 // 718-692-2828

www.ibm.com/shop

www.idot.com (preconfigured/custom PCs)

www.intellesale.com
IntellSale
510 Ryerson Road, Lincoln Park, NJ 08052
888-742-5239 // 973-686-9100

www.mei-microcenter.com
MEI-Micro Center
888-621-3927

www.micronpc.com
Micron Electronics, Inc.
888-262-1311

www.micropro.com (computers)
Micro Pro
800-353-3003 // 216-661-7218

www.notebooksuperstore.com (laptops)

www.nutrend.com (computer systems)
NuTrend
1295 Johnson Drive, City of Industry, CA 91745
888-482-6678

www.pcconnection.com (custom PCs)

www.quantex.com
Quantex Microsystems, Inc.
400B Pierce St., Somerset, NJ 08873
800-836-0566

www.sagernotebook.com (notebooks)
800-669-1624

www.shopprostar.com (laptops)
Pro Star Computers, Inc.
1126 Coiner Court, City of Industry, CA 91748
800-243-5654

www.sonydirect.com (laptops, etc.)
877-600-9367

www.store.apple.com (Apple computers)

www.tristatecomputer.com (laptops)
Tristate Computer
650 6th Ave., New York City, NY 10011
800-433-5199 // 212-633-2530

www.unitedmicro.com
United Micro
5835 Harper Rd., Solon, OH 44139
800-943-7255

www.usedcomputer.com

SOFTWARE

www.adobe.com (Pagemaker, Photoshop, etc.)
Adobe Systems, Inc.
345 Park Ave., San Jose, CA 95110
800-833-6687 // 408-536-6000

www.accountingshop.com (business software)

www.acdsystems.com (ACD See image viewing software)
ACD Systems
2201 N. Collins, #100, Arlington, TX 76011
250-382-5828

www.asymetrix.com/
Asymetrix (e-learning solutions)
110-110th Avenue N.E., Suite 700, Bellevue, WA 98004
800-448-6543 // 425-462-0501

www.autodesk.com (AutoCAD, 3D Studio drafting, etc.)
Autodesk, Inc.
111 McInnis Parkway, San Rafael, CA 94903
510-523-5900

www.beyond.com (PC/Apple software)

www.bookmarksoftware.com

www.borland.com/
Borland (distributed application development tools)
100 Enterprise Way , Scotts Valley, CA 95066
831-431-1000

www.buyonet.com (traditional/downloadable)

www.cadalog.com (CAD shareware/information)

www.caddepot.com (CAD shareware/information)

www.cai.com (anti-virus software)
Computer Associates International
One Computer Associates Plaza, Islandia, NY 11749
800-225-5224 // 631-342-5224

www.cdw.com (software)
CDW Computer Centers
200 N. Milwaukee Ave., Vernon Hills, IL 60061
800-279-4239

www.chilipepperpc.com

www.chumbo.com (traditional/downloadable)

www.Citrix.com
Citrix Systems Inc. (application server software)
6400 NW 6th Way, Fort Lauderdale, FL 33309
954-267-3000

www.Click2Learn.com
Click2Learn.com (e-learning solutions)
110 - 110th Avenue N.E., Suite 700, Bellevue, WA 98004
800-448-6543 // 425-462-0501

www.computercomputer.com (over 100,000 titles)

www.corel.com (CorelDRAW, PhotoPaint, etc.)
Corel Corporation
1600 Carling Ave., Ottawa Ontario K1Z 8R7, Canada
613-728-8200

www.cougarmtn.com (business software)
Cougar Mountain Software
7180 Potomac Drive, Suite D, Boise, ID 83704
800-388-3038

www.cws.internet.com (downloadable/updatable)

www.download.com (shareware/freeware)

www.email.com (shareware/freeware)

www.freewarefiles.com

www.futurenet.co.uk (British connection)

www.gps.com/
Great Plains (e-business solutions)
1701 SW 38th Street, Fargo, ND 58103
800-477-7736 // 701-281-6500

www.halcyon.com/knopf/distrib2.htm (shareware)

www.hotfiles.com

www.informix.com/
Informix Software, Inc. (end-to-end solutions design)
4100 Bohannon Drive, Menlo Park, CA 94025
800 331 1763 // 650 926 6300

www.inprise.com/
Inprise (Borland software)
100 Enterprise Way, Scotts Valley, CA 95066
831-431-1000

www.intuit.com/
Intuit Inc.(personal/business financial software)
2535 Garcia Avenue, Mountain View, CA 94043
650-944-6000

www.iss3.com (security software)
International Software Solutions
274 Coalisland Rd., Dungannon, Co Tyrone, Northern Ireland BT71 6ET

www.jumbo.com (shareware, etc.)

www.marimba.com/
Marimba, Inc. (Internet infrastructure management solutions)
440 Clyde Ave., Mountain View, CA 94043
650 930-5282

www.mcafee.com (antivirus software)

www.nai.com (McAfee anti-virus software, PGP encryption software)
Network Associates
3965 Freedom Circle, Santa Clara, CA 95054
972-308-9960

www.nolo.com (legal specials)

www.parsonstech.com/
Parson's
One Martha's Way, Hiawatha, Iowa 52233
319-395-9626

www.soft4u.com (business, educational, etc.)

www.softwarebuyline.com (PC/Apple/Linux)

www.software-depot.netscape.com (Internet-related products)

www.softwarestore.com (marketing, education, etc.)

www.solomon.com
Solomon Software (business management and e-business software)
200 East Hardin Street, P.O. Box 414, Findlay,OH 45840
800-4SOLOMON // 419-424-0422

www.spco.com (presentation graphics)

www.store.ea.com

www.sybase.com/
Sybase, Inc. (client/server and Internet software, etc.)
6475 Christie Ave., Emeryville, CA 94608
800-8-SYBASE // 510-922-3555

www.symantec.com (Norton anti-virus software, etc.)
Symantec Corporation
20330 Stevens Creek Blvd., Cupertino, CA 95014
408-253-9600

www.tais.com/
Toshiba America, Inc. (computers, digital imaging, and network and storage products)
1251 Sixth Avenue, 41st Floor, New York, NY 10020
212 596-0600

www.tucows.com (shareware/freeware)

www.usasoft.com (applications plus marketing)

www.zdnet.com (library of downloads)

www.winfiles.com (shareware/freeware)

www.winzip.com (WinZip file compression software)
WinZip Computing, Inc.

PERIPHERALS

www.aberdeeninc.com (motherboards, etc.)
Aberdeen, Inc.
800-501-9218 //800-502-6502

www.accesscamera.com

www.accessmicro.com (almost 50,000 items)

www.apcc.com (surge protectors, etc.)
APC
888-289-2722

www.buy-atlas.com (monitors, printers, etc.)
Atlas Micro Logistic, Inc.
1302 John Reed Court, City of Industry, CA 91745
800-336-6898

www.buycomp.com

www.usacanon.com
Canon USA, Inc.

www.casedepot.com (computer cases)
Case Depot
16013 Valley View Ave., Santa Fe Springs, CA 90670
800-200-6118 // 562-404-9725

www.ctghub.com (cables)

www.codi-inc.com (portable PC carrying cases)
800-263-4462

www.computergate.com (motherboards, cables, etc.)
Computergate International
2960 Gordon Ave., Santa Clara, CA 95051
888-437-0895

www.crutchfield.com

www.cyberwarehouse.com (monitors)
CyberWarehouse
800-792-2923

www.dirtcheapdrives.com (drives, duplicators, etc.)
Dirt Cheap Drives
800-475-7476

www.electronics.net

www.epson.com
Epson (computing and imaging products)
3840 Kilroy Airport Way, Long Beach, CA 90806
562.981.3840

www.ericsson.com/
Ericsson Inc. (cellular phones)
7001 Development Drive
Research Triangle Park, NC 27709
919-472-7000

www.56k.com (56k modems)

www.harmonycomputers.com (monitors, printers, etc.)
Harmony Computers
1801 Flatbush Ave., Brooklyn, NY 11210
800-870-1663 // 718-692-2828

Hewlett-Packard (printers, scanners, etc.)
3000 Hanover St., Palo Alto, CA 94304
650-857-1501

www.igo.com (batteries)
iGo Corporation
800-825-0293

www.imation.com/
Imation Enterprises Corp. (data storage/information management, etc.)
1 Imation Place, Oakdale, MN 55128
888-466-3456

www.interpromicro.com (drives, motherboards, etc.)
InterPro
44920 Osgood Road, Fremont CA 94539
800-226-7216 // 510-226-7226

www.iomega.com
Iomega (personal storage devices)
1821 W. Iomega Way, Roy, Utah 84067
801-332-1000

www.kingston.com (turbochips)
Kingston Technology
17600 Newhope St., Fountain Valley, CA 92708
800-588-5370 / 714-435-2600

www.lexmark.com/
Lexmark International, Inc. (printers, etc.)
Dept. 451 Bldg. 5, 740 W. New Circle Rd., Lexington, KY 40550
606-232-6537

www.megahaus.com (drives)
MegaHaus
800-786-1153

www.memory4less.com (memory modules)
Memory 4 Less
2622 W. Lincoln Ave., Suite 104, Anaheim, CA 92801
800-821-3354 // 714-826-5981

www.motherboardexpress.com (motherboards)
Motherboard Express
333 W. State Rd., Island Lake, IL 60042
888-935-4629

www.motorola.com
Motorola (phones, etc.)
1303 E. Algonquin Road, Schaumburg, IL 60196
847-576-5000

www.nectech.com
NEC Technologies (monitors, etc.)
1250 N. Arlington Heights Rd., Itasca, IL 60143
800-632-4636

www.nokia.com
Nokia (mobile phones)
6000 Connection Drive, Irving, TX 75039
972-894-5000

www.palm.com/
Palm, Inc. (handheld devices)
5400 Bayfront Plaza, Santa Clara, CA 95052
408-326-5000

www.palmcase.com (portable PC carrying cases)
781-871-7050

www.pcprogress.com
PC Progress
1711 Elmhurst Road, Elk Grove Village, IL 60007
888-727-7647 // 847-593-7450

www.plextor.com (CD-ROMs)
Plextor Corp.
800-886-3935

www.port.com (portable PC carrying cases)
800-242-3133

www.qualcomm.com/
Qualcomm (wireless devices)
5775 Morehouse Drive, San Diego, CA 92121
858-587-1121

www.quantum.com/
Quantum Corporation (data storage and information management)
500 McCarthy Blvd., Milpitas, CA 95035
408-894-4000

www.samsung.com/
www.samsungelectronics.com
Samsung Inc. (digital technology products)
105 Challenger Road Ridgefield Park, NJ 07660
800-726-7864 // 201-229-5000

www.sel.sony.com (monitors, etc.)
Sony Electronics
888-476-6972

www.spartantech.com
Spartan Technologies, Inc.
531 W. Golf Rd., Arlington Heights, IL 60005
888-373-0340

www.targus.com (portable PC carrying cases)
877-482-7487

www.tek.com/
Tektronix, Inc (test, measurement and monitoring equipment for global communications networks)
14200 SW Karl Braun Drive, P. O. Box 500, Beaverton, OR 97077
800-835-9433

www.tcwo.com
Thompson's Computer Warehouse
6306 Benjamin Rd., Suite 616, Tampa, FL 33634
800-394-4503

www.3com.com/
3COM
5400 Bayfront Plaza, Santa Clara, CA 95052
408-326-5000

www.totalcase.com (portable PC carrying cases)
877-789-0852

www.tccomputers.com (drives, memory, etc.)
Treasure Chest Computers
800-677-9781

www.tristatecomputer.com (monitors, printers, etc.)
Tristate Computer
650 6th Ave., New York City, NY 10011
800-433-5199 // 212-633-2530

www.wdc.com/
Western Digital Corporation (data storage and information management)
8105 Irvine Center Drive, Irvine, California 92618
949-932-5000

www.wirelessdimension.com (cellular phones, etc.)

INTERNET SITES
(can include sites that sell all of the above categories)

www.aberdeeninc.com (technical information; discounts)

www.aiyamicro (PC products)

www.amazon.com (books, software, etc.)

www.anything.com (over 150,000 products)

www.anythinginc.com (PC, Apple, Unix, etc.)

www/applied-computer.com (products; consultation)

www.atomicpc.com (products plus charities)

att.com/
AT&T Corporation
32 Avenue of the Americas, New York City, NY 10013
212-387-5400

www.barnesandnoble.com (books, software, etc.)

www.bell-atl.com/
Bell Atlantic Corporation
1095 Avenue of the Americas, New York City, New York 10036
800-621-9900 // 212-395-2121

www.bestprice.com (free shipping on many products)

www.bidfind.com (auctions)

www.bottomdollar.com (price comparisons)

www.buynowcomputers.com (PCs; Apple)

www.cc-inc.com

www.clubcomputer.com (includes furniture)

www.cnet.shopper.com

www.compusa.net

www.computercomputer.com (complete systems)

www.computershopper.com (good search engine)

www.dealpilot.com (books, movies, etc.)

www.ebay.com (auctions)

www.egghead.com

www.firstsource.com

www.greatcircle.com (firewall information)

www.imc.org/
Internet Mail Consortium (helps manage and promote the expanding world of electronic mail)
127 Segre Place, Santa Cruz, CA 95060
831-426-9827

www.lsoft.com/lists/LIST_Q (database of mailing lists)

www.neosoft.com/internet/paml (database of mailing lists)

www.onsale.com

www.pcmall.com (peripherals, notebooks, etc.)
PC Mall
800-932-2602

www.powells.com (books, etc.)

www.qwest.com/
Qwest (broadband Internet-based communications)
555 17th Street, Denver, CO 80202
800-899-7780 // 303-992-1400

www.shopping.com

www.shoppingplanet.com

www.sprint.com/
Sprint (telecommunications need)
2330 Shawnee Mission Parkway, Westwood, KS 66205
913-624-3000

www.surplusauction.com

www.techweb.com/shopper

www.varsitybooks.com
Industry, CA 91745
800-336-6898

www.warehouse.com (gift with every order)

www.wcom.com
MCI/WorldComm (communications services)
500 Clinton Center Drive, Clinton, MS 39056
877-624-9266 // 601-460-5600

www.w3.org/
World Wide Web Consortium (standards group for keeping HTML code open and free)
MIT, Laboratory for Computer Science, 545 Technology Square, Cambridge, MA 02139
617-253-2613

www.xerox.com
Xerox (copiers, document imaging)
800 Long Ridge Road, P.O. Box 1600, Stamford, CT 06904
203-968-3000

Index